PUBLISHED IN JUNE 2018

THE TITLE, STYLE OF MAKE-U
ALMANACK ARE STRI

Foulsham's
OLD MO   S
ALMANACK

1697   THE ORIGINAL COPYRIGHT EDITION   2019

2019 – The Year for

Optimistic Rebuilding

All change! That's what we should expect in 2019. So, I am calling it the year for self-reliance. The UK is some way down its own path to making changes. So, the year will have fewer surprises for us than it may for others. The world has been slow to change and Pluto, the *changer*, is impatient.

The West opens with high expectations. Early in the year, the influence of Jupiter and Neptune will generate optimism and the feeling that we *can* overcome our struggles. One of the most exciting planetary changes of the year will be made by Chiron, the healer. It moves, full-time, into pioneering Aries. On the last two occasions that it was there we went through the Roaring Twenties and the 'Me-Decade' starting early in the 1970s. It was party time and the world was very relaxed! The UK deserves a party, so looking at this one, I won't dampen too much. But while we are relaxed, the rest of the world should not be. They will have to start to deal with their own problems this year.

Chiron works slowly and always ends up being very disruptive of the establishment that it finds. What is the establishment it finds? Above all, the world is full of mature money systems, that have been deeply abused and are heavily in debt. Following the 2008 financial crisis, we decided to correct our own situation and this produced the hardships we have been through. Too many other governments chose to avoid this, but their time must come. The world needs to return to living within its means, as we have been trying to do. The

Tel: (01628) 400631
The Old Barrel Store,
Drayman's Lane,
Marlow, Bucks SL7 2FF

Pluto influence will make the world face-up to its money problems, clear out its corrup management and rebuild honest systems.

Through the year, I see international financial scenes of conflict between the self-interests o the elite and the expectations of the people. I am looking for the exposure of practices that are shaming. The culprits will be in Banks, Governments and Financial Regulators that have not beer through correction. Pluto will continue to bring theirs about. The world needs to put its worst times behind it, and rediscover the honest values that everybody truly wants to be returned.

I will be looking for demonstrations of this in a move by electorates towards Populis Leaders. Voters will be looking for politics that are untainted by a history of corruption. They will want newer parties, perceived to be closer to the people. These are hopeful votes, looking for more honest, humanitarian government. There will be a sense that enough is enough, and that politicians must accept that a new way is dawning. Politics will become more 'amateur across Europe, employment will rise and some economic strength will be recovered.

In my deeper studies of 2019, I found myself looking at America more often than is usual. It suffers from so many of the underlying symptoms that I talk of here. There are signs that beneath its encouraging output and growth, severe economic problems are still building. Whatever kind of positive mood we can create for *ourselves*, it looks like their authority will be losing its grip. Right now, instead of managing its financial crisis, more and more fake money is being printed to buy off an inevitable crash. Chiron's method of work is to progressively encourage such abuses, until it forces a collapse. In 2019, I am looking for the beginning of its monetary disruption.

Just as money seems to be disrupted in 2019, so too will be the pace of change in the work place. We should expect the growth of inexpensive technology in business and finance. I expect to see a new generation of software coming to work. It contains Artificial Intelligence, which will raise questions about the unemployment that it may produce. Uranus, through Taurus the 'builder' will further expand these technologies, and its impact will be much more than simple *modernising*. Taurus changes our economic *behaviour*. I see this producing a significant rise in the acceptance of E-currencies.

It is difficult to be sure if this is because of serious concern for the long-term value of paper monies. Or, if there is a wider understanding of this new values system. The critical difference between the two is that paper money is manipulated by International Financial Managers who have lost the trust of their communities while E-currencies, such as Bit Coin, have no central management, because it was designed to work beyond the grasp of abusive management.

In the background, this year is being driven by Pluto, a massive transformer, even revolutionary. So, the year is, essentially, anti-establishment and correcting imbalance. Pluto produces *demolished endings*, to leave new, *principled beginnings* in its wake. In the knowledge that we have the best of it, I wish you all a happy and settled year, dear reader.

Dr Francis Moore, September 2017

1 to 9
Numbers and Their Amazing Effect on Luck

f you can count from 1 to 9 you can use this book! 'All luck revolves around numbers!', declares J. deVille, author. Each hour, day and date is governed by one of the nine numbers, be it the 9th or the 27th.

Why will something be successful one day, but not the next? 'Because of numbers!' he says. 'When the wrong number is chosen – which is usually the case – the chances of success are only 1 in 9', he opines. 'You are usually therefore more likely to fail 9 times out of 10 – but that ratio can be turned on its head!' he declares.

'THE DIFFERENCE BETWEEN A SUCCESSFUL SURGICAL OPERATION AND A FAILURE', he believes, 'COULD ALL BE DOWN TO THE HOUR AND THE DATE!'

Of course, dates are given to us over which we have no control – the author shows how to circumvent this problem.

'Numbers are more vital than astrology, biorhythms and other cyclic processes', he claims. 'They dominate our lives and most of us never know it.' The author's first address was at No. 7; he began primary school on the 7th and entered college on the 25th (2+5=7); got married on the 14th (twice 7); and so on – 'and yet if I use 7 to bring me luck it won't work. So-called "lucky numbers" are another matter altogether!'

He continues: 'If you have not been lucky it may be because you have not done things at the right time, not because you are a fool.'

'I will show you once and for all what your propitious numbers could be – and not what you think they are!'

No rituals required! No visualisation or applied concentration! You need only to be able to count from 1 to 9 (numbers above that are irrelevant). We are restricted to what claims can be made for this book, but we can cite a few of its chapter headings: The Luck & Significance of Numbers; Improving Business; Successful Timing; The Woman Who Found Herself A Husband; Names & Places Have Numbers; The Man Who Lived Off Gambling; Cycles.

To receive the book '1 to 9: Numbers & Their Amazing Effect On Luck', please send **£9.99** cheque or postal order, payable to 'Finbarr', to: Finbarr, (O19), Folkestone CT20 2QQ. Overseas send £15.99 to cover air mail. Major cards accepted, please give number, start date, expiry date & last three digits or security number on back of card. If in a hurry please add 80p & write 'PRIORITY' on face of envelope for extra fast delivery. Catalogue of unusual books 95p. PLEASE DON'T FORGET TO GIVE YOUR NAME AND ADDRESS!

DEFEATING DEPRESSION

5 words changed my life!' claims author Deborah Anderson. 20 years of depression lifted! Not a prayer, not a chant. Information here not found elsewhere. Essential reading for those who have tried the usual treatments and failed. **£9.99** from: Finbarr (OD), Folkestone, Kent CT20 2QQ. Overseas £14.99.

NEW SALT MAGIC RITES

Chapters include: **Salt Magic Brings Money – Influencing Another Person's Thoughts & Actions – Salt Rites to Protect Against Physical Injury – Salt Rite To Get A Job.** Are you aware that sprinkling salt outside your front door could keep unwanted persons away? Everything is explained in this volume. Also details for sprinkling salt on important documents and lottery coupons. Common salt from your supermarket is all you need. Note these unsolicited testimonials (copies of originals available on request): 'Have already had two wins on the pools' (M.B., Fleetwood): 'In ten minutes my violent son quietened down ... have had no trouble from him since' (P.E., Manchester); 'IT REALLY WORKS! I won £1411' (A.P., Grimsby); 'Since I got your book ... money has come into my home in different ways ... my son has paid off his debts ... I bless the day I sent for this book (D.L., Hove) – this same lady wrote again five months later: 'The salt rites are still working for us ... every day we receive something good!' To receive 'New Salt Magic Rites' please send £9.99 to: Finbarr (OS), Folkestone, Kent CT20 2QQ (address complete) Overseas send £14.99.

Lost Magick Rites
From the Archives of Finbarr

Winning Court Cases!
Getting Someone Out Of Your Life!

Bringing Back Someone!

Magick rites from long out-of-print books by Marcus Bottomley and Frank Gupta, copyright Finbarr, made available in one volume!

In response to demand from serious collectors of magical lore we are publishing this work of *authentic magick rites.*

Magick rites that allegedly influence the outcome of court hearings! Magick rites which, allegedly, sway witnesses and judges! 'With magick, a case is won before the parties even appear in court', claims author.

Magick rites which allegedly *compel* another to leave!

Magick rites which allegedly can break up another's love affair.

Magick rites which shield and protect the magician from harm.

This is the only book to contain these particularly rare and sought after rites!

There's a magick rite here which allegedly cures male impotency.

A magick rite for allegedly uncovering the identity of a thief.

A magick rite for allegedly punishing an enemy.

Magick rites which allegedly make an estranged lover contact you, or return.

A magick rite which allegedly identifying the person one will marry.

Magick rites which allegedly place another under one's control.

Magick rites which allegedly control the forces of luck, influencing the outcome of gambling; increasing one's fortune in business.

Magick rites which allegedly sever a relationship.

Magick rites which allegedly enables one to find a job/promotion.

Magick rites which allegedly influence employers.

A magick rite which reverses curses; restoring good fortune.

A magick rite which allegedly controls ghosts and malicious spirits.

These are the magick rites we have been asked time and again to publish, for the benefit of all collectors of magickal lore.

Magick rites which allegedly increase mental powers, improving concentration and memory.

Aphrodisiac magick! – Magick for acquiring riches! – Magick for peace and harmony in the home! – Voodoo money, luck and subjugation spells!

For the serious collector, this is a goldmine of rare and closely guarded folk magick; only Finbarr holds the copyright. Despite the potency attached to these rites some are remarkably easy to do.

Strange powers are attributed to these magick rites.

These rites have been passed by word of mouth, generation to generation under oaths of secrecy, through the long passages of time. Only Finbarr possesses their printed copyright.

These are the magick rites used by professional occultists who, for substantial fees, offer their services to those in need.

These magick rites allegedly give the reader/practitioner strange powers over circumstances and people. According to the authors this is 'real' magick: not dependent on visualization or positive thinking. 'Science cannot explain it and never will', they say.

To receive LOST MAGICK RITES FROM THE ARCHIVES OF FINBARR please send £9.99 to: Finbarr (OL), Folkestone, CT20 2QQ. Overseas £15.99.

2019 – World Preview

There are three eclipses to note this year and these take place in January, July and December the middle being a total solar eclipse. In August 2017 (in Leo) it caused ripples and a downright scandal in the Hollywood entertainment industry. This time (in Cancer) a prominent family or property magnate may come under scrutiny. Eclipses breed uncertainty but can indicate situations coming to an end, followed by a new beginning. This may occur in Western politics, with a new controversy regarding a prominent world leader; eclipses have a way of revealing unpalatable truths.

THE ECONOMY

World economies have been enjoying a phase of simultaneous growth, with increases in GDP and falling unemployment, whether across the Eurozone, the UK, America, Canada or China. Economic expansion is the key phrase in 2019 as Jupiter and Neptune make strong contacts in the months of January, May and September, any of which may coincide with over-optimism and high expectations, instability and 'overheating' of the economy.

This Jupiter effect means that in 2019 inflation will be on the rise. There may eventually be a fall out in the markets, and speculative bubbles are likely to burst in the latter half of the year. Coupled with reduced liquidity this could presage a sell-off in equities when the damage to investor confidence could be huge. For example, the Dollar could be under severe pressure in September, struggling somewhat against the Euro.

UNITED KINGDOM

Jupiter will strongly influence the United Kingdom chart at key points in 2019, suggesting a sure-footed government pressing ahead with policies, even though some will be deeply unpopular. This will show how self-confidence can look like arrogance. In January and June we may see new optimistic projects announced in transport, especially the rail and aeronautics industries. This is underlined by the strong presence of belligerent Mars in 2019 indicating an aggressive stance in any foreign diplomacy and negotiations, in particular the ones from Brexit.

There are notes of optimism and economic growth in early 2019, this in spite of Brexit. Jupiter's alignment with the Moon is good news for schools, the NHS, tourism and the service industries. However, the influence of Saturn on the Tory party chart in June suggests the leadership is under mounting pressure, directly connected to the handling of Britain leaving the European Union. On the UK chart, Pluto makes another significant alignment which suggests there could be a change of resident in Number 10 by mid-summer.

EUROPE

The next elections for the European Parliament will occur around 23–26 May 2019, shortly after the deadline for Britain leaving the EU. These will have a deep impact on the future course of Europe. A planetary alignment between Uranus and the Moon indicates some shocks and surprises after conventional expectations go awry. The EU Parliament will thereafter feature a considerable collection of Eurosceptics.

German politics is also undergoing a transformation – it is undergoing its 'Saturn return' after the unification 29 years ago. This means it will have to rethink – even abandon – certain policies on EU integration which have since proven unrealistic. The EU will have to be more conciliatory and co-operative with the new right wing parties on the scene: in Germany, the Czech Republic, Austria and Hungary. Plus there may be unrest in southern Europe during the summer, a situation that may escalate into a civil war.

USA

America is in an especially bullish phase in 2019 as Jupiter passes through a critical place on the US National Chart. It is facing the rest of the world with a heightened sense of complacency. This may also coincide with a resurgent military build-up in the Army, Air Force and Navy. However, self-confidence may be dented in 2019 as the US economy comes under the threat of recession. The cycles applying to the US this year suggest a slowdown in recent growth which is bad news for the economy, and if this starts to founder, so does the President's popularity.

There are any number of real world influences that could presage the indicated recession: the Democrats might precipitate an impeachment process, or inflation may spike. At any rate, planetary stresses from Saturn on Donald Trump's birth chart in 2019 show he'll have difficulty playing the maverick and popular confounder of expectations, as July's solar eclipse also affects his chart. This may coincide with a new scandal – for example an FBI investigation could take a disconcerting turn. However, this may not be sufficient to kick start the impeachment that many Democrats would like to see.

RUSSIA AND CHINA

Mars has been crossing a critical point on Russia's chart for a number of years, which is why the West increasingly sees it as belligerent and warlike, and even criminal. This phase will peak in mid-2020, but up until then the country will seem like a rogue state to many. Expect little change in 2019 as Putin consolidates his hold on power – bolstered by Jupiter, Saturn and Pluto. There may be new sanctions on Russia so expect reports of skullduggery in foreign trade deals when Putin retaliates.

China, the most spectacular economic/political sensation of recent times, is also feeling confident on the world stage as the combined effect of Pluto and Jupiter make it a massive economic powerhouse of production. However, in the financial markets this can mean instability and the Chinese debt bubble may burst in 2019.

Meghan Markle

© PA Images

The Royal Wedding between Prince Harry and Meghan Markle took place on 19 May 2018 at Windsor Castle. Meghan is a woman of many talents: actor, life-coach, graduate of the illustrious Northwestern University in the USA, and a tireless philanthropist with a history of charity work for women's causes. She even ran her own lifestyle website. From the day of her engagement, Meghan became the new darling of the tabloids and excitement around her star-studded, fairytale wedding saw her popularity soar. What everyone wants to know now, is how the marriage will work out and will she fit into the British Royal family?

Meghan was born on 4 August 1981 in Los Angeles, California at 4.46 am: a proud, sunny Leo with an emotional and sensitive Cancerian ascendant, and her Moon in amicable Libra. That Sun (along with communicative Mercury) is in the first house (personality) of her chart, so she's going to make us all take notice, with that powerful impact that Leos have. The key to her real character is the Moon–Jupiter–Saturn alignment in Libra. This makes her emotionally quite guarded, with a serious, ambitious, singularity of purpose – she knows what she wants from life and won't settle for second best.

As we look at the cross-connections between Meghan's and Harry's birth charts, we see that Meghan may turn the Prince's world upside down, especially in how he relates to emotional issues. If there is any kernel of tension it's that her chart reveals that she requires plenty of personal freedom. Her new Royal role has meant giving up her previous charity and ambassadorial work and taking on new causes, which may take some getting used to. If Meghan makes a stand and retains an element of her previous independence, Harry may become rather impatient. Meghan's Venus powerfully aspects Harry's Uranus – always an alignment that evokes issues of personal space and freedom within a partnership.

In another configuration with romantic Venus, bold Mars and dreamy Neptune indicate that strong passions are stirred between them – everything is intensified to the max. Planetary positions suggest that any teething problems in the first couple of years of the marriage are likely come in June and July 2019, when the Uranus factor is strong. Meghan may want the independence to use her creativity. Another period of internal pressure arises in December. Fortunately, the astrological indicators in the relationship are strong. Learning to conform to Royal protocol would be a challenge for any woman who married Prince Harry but this couple's charts clearly reveal a spirit of 'us against the world', and with mutual emotional support, this is the perfect attitude.

9

Jodie Whittaker

© PA Images

English-born actress Jodie Whittaker was born in Yorkshire on 3 January 1982. Her astrological chart shows that she was destined to be in the public eye from a very early age. Jodie has her Sun and the planet Mercury in quiet Capricorn but this gives her determination and the sort of staying power necessary to stick at building a stage, television and film career that has gone from strength to strength.

Like many actors, Jodie began her career on the stage. She won awards during her training and showed a great deal of promise. The silver screen first came calling in 2006 with a role in the film *Venus*. Almost everything in Jodie's birth chart is 'over' the Earth, which itself can indicate fame. Her natural raw talent is overlaid with great sensitivity, which comes from Jupiter in Scorpio; her undoubted adaptability is thanks to Venus in Aquarius and an unusual streak comes from several different planetary positions and their relationship with each other.

Despite Jodie's many successes, on TV in series such as *Broadchurch* and *Cranford* and in plays like *The Seagull*, Jodie is currently enjoying a new level of fame on account of a role she has barely yet played at all: the thirteenth incarnation of Dr Who – the first woman to be cast in this seminal role. Her chart reveals that she is ideally suited for this part, not only in terms of her acting talent but also because quirky Aquarius is so strong in her chart and also on account of Mars in Libra, which tells us that she will cope with any leftover machismo that may have become attached to the role.

Jodie's individuality shines out through most aspects of her natal chart and this comes through in her personality. Although friendly and approachable Jodie Whittaker is no pushover, and with odd Uranus in Sagittarius she may use some fairly unorthodox and very original strategies to keep her life on course. Above all, her Sun in Capricorn ensures she is grounded in the real world and gives her a robust constitution. As Dr Who she is likely to win great acclaim, almost certainly to the extent that she will bring round any critics of a woman playing this role.

Look out for a really big international film role for Jodie in the not-too-distant future, together with the chance of television work in a capacity that she had not handled before – perhaps as a presenter. Eventually, we may see her turn in a political direction as her chart demonstrates that the older she grows the deeper will become her convictions and the more she will seek to share her unique talents. Old Moore would not be surprised to see Jodie Whittaker become one of the most prominent celebrities of our era.

'One Spell Brought Me What I Sought'

And still continues to bring me what I want (*writes Elaine Delaney*). It has worked continuously for me. For years now it has been my comfort and hope.

When my husband didn't stand a chance against the many other candidates in line for promotion I performed this spell and he got it. And what a difference this promotion made to our household income!

This spell literally works like magic.

My daughter was seeing a lad I had grave misgivings about. This spell separated them.

When I needed a pay rise I got it, after using this spell.

You need no experience to cast this spell. And work it surely will if you follow the simple instructions in my book.

Even if you lack privacy you can still perform this spell!

How and why it works I cannot adequately explain. All that I know is that it works.

My two sisters-in-law hadn't spoken in years. This spell reconciled them. They didn't know I was behind this, but it gave me great pleasure.

The wonderful thing about this one spell is that it can be used for almost any purpose … so long as it is not used with evil intent.

Whatever you need, whatever your aim, you can turn to this spell as I have done consistently over the years.

If you desire the love and attention of someone this one spell can make your dream come true.

If you want to be rid of someone, the relationship isn't working any more … this one spell can do the trick.

Or if you want to be reunited with someone this one spell can make it happen.

If you have tried and failed with other spells then you need this one.

I have shared this spell with friends who have achieved the same wonderful results. One lady, tired of never winning a bean in any game or contest, quickly won around $1000 twice in succession after I gave her this spell.

I will tell you of a teenager who wanted the same gorgeous looking lad as a dozen others. Thanks to this spell, she was the one to get him.

It works, too, for the most mundane things. Upset that I didn't get a refund on an electrical appliance that didn't work from the start I performed the spell and hey presto! I received £374 (the full amount owed) in the post.

It seems like make-believe. Sometimes I have to pinch myself. But work it really does.

Anyone can perform it. Even the person without privacy, surrounded by nosey busybodies.

A friend was losing sleep over an obnoxious neighbour. 'If only she would move!' she said. 'Well, she could if you would try this spell', I replied.

'But how can something this easy work?'

'Don't fret or doubt this. Just do it. You have nothing to lose – but you might lose a bad neighbour!'

Within the month the neighbour was gone. My friend was so happy!

Over the years I have encountered people who tell me it's all rubbish. I let them get on with it. I know what I have experienced.

Though this one spell is so simple you still have to go about it the right way as I explain in my book.

With this spell you can avoid making the wrong decisions.

This one spell can help you make the right decision immediately on the spot.

There is nothing sinister in it and it must be only used for good. Use it regularly and it could change your life – if that's what you want.

I could not imagine my life without this spell. As I say, I find it of lasting comfort.

Whether it's life's daily little annoyances or something serious like a relationship in difficulty or a financial crisis, this one spell can smooth the way.

If you think I'm mad that's your privilege. I see the positive effects on a regular basis and I know it's not in my imagination, nor simply 'lucky coincidence'.

Yes, I believe there is a greater power around us, ready to guide and inspire if we would but let it. This spell tunes into that power.

For me this spell brings constant hope and comfort. I do not have to fret, for I have this spell at my call. Yes, I believe in 'magic': the magic of the mind, the magic of the universe. It is there all right. This spell demonstrates it.

It certainly doesn't replace all other spells, but it is the one you will return to again and again.

Please send £9.99 – payable to 'Finbarr' – to Finbarr (O), Folkestone, Kent CT20 2QQ. Overseas £14.99.
If in a hurry write 'PRIORITY' on face of envelope and add 80p for extra fast delivery. Major cards accepted.

Matt Baker

© PA Images

Television presenter and all-round action man Matt Baker was born on 23 December 1977. Although sadly we do not have his time of birth, Matt's chart reveals a great deal of information that can get us closer to a man who is becoming the nation's favourite, and who continues to take on new challenges.

Matt Baker was born with his Sun just into Capricorn by one degree, with Moon in capricious Gemini and Mercury and Venus in go-getting Sagittarius. It's action all the way for anyone who comes into the world with a chart such as this so it is no wonder that Matt accepts and completes so many physical adventures. This birth chart balances a need to be active – and to entertain – with the deep sensitivity that comes from the position of Jupiter and the aspects it has to other planets in the birth chart.

When Matt's first career choice of physiotherapy did not work out, he began his television career as a Blue Peter presenter in 1999 – and never looked back. His popularity with the viewing public was never in doubt and the Gemini and Sagittarius in his chart gives him the ability to cross the divide as far as the generations are concerned. He is most familiar to viewers these days as a co-presenter of *The One Show*, where his easy-going and humorous approach to the guests who appear nightly has won him acclaim and awards. But there is another side to Matt. Although his parents originally ran a shop in County Durham, they also had a smallholding and eventually swapped this for a farm. Matt took to working on the land like a duck to water. The Sun and Saturn both occupy Earth signs in his birth chart and it is extremely likely that his ascending sign is either Taurus or Virgo. These planetary positions made Matt a natural choice when a new presenter was needed for BBC One's phenomenally popular Sunday evening farming programme, *Countryfile*. Again equal to any challenge that comes his way, Matt travels the UK interviewing people in their home environments and participating in all manner of country activities. This love of nature and the countryside will always be an important part of Matt's makeup and in his work and his life he is unlikely to stray far from the wide open spaces that are so clearly defined in his well-spread and adaptable birth chart.

If we look ahead to what lies in store for Matt Baker in the years to come, it looks likely that he will continue to occupy our television screens for years to come. Look out for him in an acting role of some sort before long and expect him to receive a singular honour before the decade is over.

The Only Prayer You Will Ever Need

A PRAYER LIKE NO OTHER – A *PRAYER WITHOUT WORDS*

Elvira Powel writes:

I received this prayer from my uncle who was on his deathbed. I will never forget his words, 'This is the only prayer you will ever need.'

It changed my life.

I was out of a job. I had lost my home.

My health was failing

Yet this prayer changed everything.

It is worth more to me than anything money can buy, for I know that whatever I need it can supply.

It brought me hope. It even made my children better behaved!

I have always believed in prayer. But my prayers were not always answered. None of this matters now, for I now have the only prayer I will ever need.

My long night of darkness was over. Into the light I emerged and not only were problems solved but my life was at last going forward.

I found a job I love, one that is secure. And I met a wonderful man: a successful businessman who loves not only me but my children too.

I put all this down to this one prayer.

When my uncle explained it to me I was amazed. 'How can a prayer be without words?' I asked. 'Don't question it', he replied, 'just do it.'

He said, 'Even if one doesn't believe in the God of the Church it will work for you. *Just do it!*'

I had never known anything like it.

It takes only moments and can be used by anyone of any faith or religion.

And it has inspired me to write this book. The publisher tried this prayer and tells me that he now uses it every day. 'I will not argue with what your uncle said, "the only prayer you will ever need". I am amazed by it and the immediate help it has given me for many situations.'

Whatever your need, use this prayer.

If you need more money, use this prayer.

If you need to solve an intractable problem, use this prayer.

If you need love, use this prayer.

If you want someone to love you again, this is the only prayer you need.

If you are ill, trust in this prayer, for your health is about to change.

My sister's life was a misery on account of so many allergies. This prayer changed everything. Now she enjoys life to the full.

I explained it to a young colleague who was anxious about her next driving test. She passed after using the prayer (she had failed the previous 7 times).

I could go on.

If anyone had told me previously that I could use or 'say' a prayer in which no words were spoken I would not have believed.

But because it was my uncle who told me, and I had always trusted him completely, I took his word for it.

I am so excited that I feel the whole world should know about it. I can't see why it should be kept hidden.

It is the best thing to ever happen to me. I now live in faith, for I have this prayer which unfailingly helps and guides me.

I use it daily to ensure that my day goes well. And so it does. I believe I am living a 'charmed life'; and I am so grateful. I give thanks every day and never fail to think of my dear uncle in spirit.

This prayer brings immediate comfort. You feel good the moment you use it, and you feel even better when you see the results you've been hoping for.

No matter what your circumstances, no matter how low you've been, I want you to know that right now *there is real hope.*

I know some will laugh at me, but I don't care. I have all the proof I will ever need. And I keep on getting the proof – every day.

It is the prayer that 'moves mountains', lifts the spirit, and dissolves obstacles.

I know now that my health will always be perfect.

I know now that I will never lack for anything again.

I live in a state of complete reassurance.

This is not to say I am smug. Perish the thought. After what I've been through I am just *so grateful.*

I don't have to worry about my children or anyone else close to me. I use this prayer for them and I just *know* it is answered.

If you need a better memory, better concentration, more confidence, more money, a better job, a promotion, gambling wins – whatever – this prayer will answer your need.

Because it is so simple it does not mean it is not powerful. Probably the reason it has been kept concealed is precisely because it is both simple and potent. I cannot for the life of me see why anything so good should not be available to all.

If you believe, you will be thrilled by the results.

You will then say, like me, that it is the only prayer you will ever need.

Brexit and the Economy in 2019
What Next for Britain?

In 2016 the British people were asked in a referendum whether they wanted to stay in, or leave, the European Union. As we all know, 52% voted to leave and on 29 March 2017 the Prime Minister penned the historic letter to Donald Tusk informing him of Britain's intention to leave the EU and triggering the Brexit process. Following a two-year notice period, Britain will do just that on 29 March 2019. What kind of conditions should we expect? What do the planetary alignments indicate for Britain and its economy in the wake of Brexit? Important issues at stake include the Northern Ireland border, the arrangements governing European travel, what immigration will look like and – crucially – how British business and the economy will perform. The question is: will we be better or worse off?

DEAL OR NO DEAL?

The kind of deal we negotiate with the rest of Europe, the so-called 'soft' or 'hard' exit, is the subject of endless debate. We know that if a new deal is not agreed to replace or extend our membership of the single market, Britain's future trade with the EU will be on WTO (World Trade Organisation) terms – the same terms as those used by the rest of the world. Planetary alignments involving Saturn with the Moon on 29 March 2019 indicate an abrupt separation and tough economic times. These two planets coming together signify dogged self-reliance, wilful isolation even, making the WTO option a likely outcome.

THE EXIT POLL CHART

The chart at the time that the polls closed on referendum day reveal that powerful Pluto was sitting on the Capricorn ascendant. This indicates the scope of Brexit's ambition, but also divisive vested interests determined to have their own way. And so we have seen little sense of working *together* to move forward in the national interest, even within the Conservative party, where members divide on Leave/Remain lines. A Mars alignment with the MC (the 'public face') lies behind this combative nature whilst revolutionary Uranus makes a harsh contact to Pluto. These are energies for change and rebirth that manifest erratically – pointing to unforeseen administrative and practical difficulties, whether in EU talks or Parliament. Expect these to deepen in May and June.

THE ARTICLE 50 CHART

The birth chart for the triggering of Brexit itself, appropriately, has Pluto (political power) contacting Jupiter (high ambition). Article 50 is a key document in British political history and its chart with erratic and unpredictable Moon–Mercury–Uranus contact in feisty Aries suggests impatience, hot tempers and unexpected diversions. This is manifested in the deadlock between the EU and Brexit negotiators. Fortunately, a helpful aspect from earthy, practical Saturn should stabilise matters and keep them on course.

Staid Saturn and ambitious Jupiter make an uneasy planetary alliance in June and December, which is bad news for economic growth, exports and employment. Brexit will certainly drag on the economy, making it slower. However, in 2019 what astrologers call a Grand Trine (for harmony) occurs between three key planets (involving Jupiter and Mars) which suggests we'll see the government make the best of a bad economic situation, despite inflation and the threat of rising interest rates.

WILL WE REJOIN THE EU?

This is the question that won't go away as Remainers struggle to see a future for the UK outside the EU. Will there come a time when we reverse Brexit and rejoin the EU at a later date? For Leavers the prospect is unthinkable, but the question is worth asking given that some polls since the referendum have indicated a slight change in voting choices, with fewer people claiming that they would now vote Leave. Rejoining, presumably, couldn't happen without a change of government, and next British General Election is not due until 5 May 2022. It is possible, of course, that events within the Conservative party, including a new leader, or pressure put upon it from Parliament might bring this date forward, but for now planetary configurations for that date show the influence of Saturn (in late April around election time) which says: 'security first', or 'don't risk anything new' and a firm attachment to tradition and the past, all of which indicates no change of government, irrespective of whether or not Theresa May is still in Number 10.

All the main charts reveal difficulties in getting along with our fellow Europeans, with nothing to suggest a second referendum. It seems that, to echo Mrs May, Brexit means Brexit! But how will the Tories fulfill their promise to get us the best deal from Brexit? The planetary picture on the Conservative party chart for March 2019 shows incredible pressure from taskmaster Saturn. The government will have plenty of obstacles to surmount from Europe and the Remain camp, both within and outside its own ranks, possibly some that are very unexpected. The disagreements and in-fighting may be so great within the party that by June a leadership election is the only eventual recourse.

Old Moore understands that the presence of self-reliant Saturn on all the significant charts is the undercurrent of the Brexit process. It brings strong independence and national pride, and inflexibility, too. The effect of Jupiter and Neptune brings high expectations and inflated ideals, but some of these ideals cannot manifest as hoped for – Saturn always provides a reality check! At the end of the day, we seem to be looking at a *hard Brexit*. But those who fear this must realise that there is light at the end of the tunnel. There are promising signs of growth for later in 2019, with 'home-grown' jobs, such as tourism and the service industry well aspected. In time, with more money available, underfunded public services may benefit from higher budget allocations. Britain keeps calm, and carries on.

Your 2019 Birthday Guide

By working with the major astrological influences, you can take control and give your life a better focus. These personal guides show you how to make the most of the positive times and also indicate which days need to be handled with care.

ARIES BORN PEOPLE

Birthdays: 21 March to 20 April inclusive
Planet: Mars. Birthstone: Diamond. Lucky day: Tuesday

Keynote for the Year: *This year should see you broadening your horizons as long-range travel is very well highlighted in your chart. Career wise, a time to reap the harvest of previous hard work.*

JANUARY: MAIN TRENDS: 7–8 Debates and discussions should be stimulating as you enjoy the chance to chew over and consider valuable ideas. **22–23** Personal relationships are on a roll and you are in most people's good books. A great time to meet new people. **24–25** Practical matters should progress productively and there may now be scope for real improvement in your professional life. **KEY DATES: HIGHS 19–20** Expect to have a great deal of energy to throw into new projects. **LOWS 4–5** Avoid unnecessary conflicts over everyday matters that could lead to disappointment.

FEBRUARY: MAIN TRENDS: 2–3 Your strengths lie in your ability to organise things at work, and to withstand many pressures now. **12–13** Put your best foot forward and look out for various opportunities at this time – they may appear where you least expect them. **20–21** Some projects that have until now been just at the ideas stage may begin to develop into promising ventures. **KEY DATES: HIGHS 9–10** In a highly creative mood, you will function best when you are at the centre of attention. **LOWS 22–23** Be content just to get by until this potentially stressful influence passes.

MARCH: MAIN TRENDS: 1–3 Make sure that you get the best out of your domestic life; concentrating on family matters will do you the world of good. **23–24** With your enthusiasm strong, this is a good time to effect long-lasting changes in your personal life. **26–27** You may reach a minor crossroads, a professional or personal peak. Prepare to have to choose between two attractive alternatives. **KEY DATES: HIGHS 8–9** A 'green light' period when personal victory is never far away. **LOWS 21–22** At best, this should be a pretty ordinary period; at worst, there may be unheralded setbacks.

APRIL: MAIN TRENDS: 15–16 A high point for friendships and anything involving teamwork. Don't stay at home, get out and enjoy time spent with others. **20–21** Trends favour your social life, but your worldly ambitions may also come closer to fruition. **22–23** Discussions go the way you would like during this great period for all types of communication. Someone, somewhere may be inspirational. **KEY DATES: HIGHS 4–5** Trends suggest that someone you meet will favourably influence you. **LOWS 17–18** Responsibilities may interfere with your free time. Fulfil your obligations before turning to pleasurable pursuits.

MAY: MAIN TRENDS: 6–7 Take advantage of any opportunity to be on the move, travel and discover new places and people. Teamwork is also favourably highlighted. **17–18** Trends favour all forms of partnership; you may come to recognise just how valuable others are to you. **20–21** What you hear from others now could prove valuable as trends conspire to help put you in the picture. **KEY DATES: HIGHS 1–3; 29–30** With the help of some ingenious ideas, put your best foot forward and strike out for what you want. **LOWS 15–16** A 'lay off' period between major activities; take things slowly, especially at work and with finances.

JUNE: MAIN TRENDS: 4–5 The perfect time to pursue your heart's desire – your leadership abilities and competitive instincts help you to achieve your short-term goals. **9–10** At ease with life, you will enjoy entertaining at home. Relations with family members should also be more relaxed than usual. **21–22** Trends assist you to be effective in a business matter and easily able to cut through the red tape to the right moves. **KEY DATES: HIGHS 25–26** Embrace your inner extrovert and you may even stumble across some short cuts to success. **LOWS 11–12** Don't shoulder too many burdens and accept that you can't solve everything single-handedly.

JULY: MAIN TRENDS: 3–4 This trend may force you to reconsider a practical matter after a temporary lull in progress at work. **25–26** Under socially and romantically powerful trends this is a wonderful time to tell someone you love them. **28–29** A mental and physical peak when positive action may provide a sensible solution to a long-standing problem. **KEY DATES: HIGHS 22–24** Expect the best from life and you may see a golden opportunity for personal development. **LOWS 8–9** Consult others on important decisions, as your capacity for sound judgement may be impaired now.

AUGUST: MAIN TRENDS: 11–12 Trends favour your private life so enjoy some happy encounters with old faces and look for fresh insight into old matters. **17–18** Communications flow smoothly and quickly. You may learn something useful or receive news that excites you into action. **23–24** Business ideas and initiatives are likely to receive a thumbs-up. Your income may increase if your competitive skills give you the edge at work. **KEY DATES: HIGHS 19–21** Life looks bright and Lady Luck favours you under these sunny trends. **LOWS 5–6** Spirits may sag a little as a lack of direction sets you back somehow.

SEPTEMBER: MAIN TRENDS: 13–14 Trends assist you to find support in your endeavours, and lend you a little luck, too. **15–16** Your professional life is rewarding; you should make progress with your plans and might even take a step up the ladder! **23–24** Beneficial trends highlight social matters now and if you're seeking friendship you can't go wrong at this time. **KEY DATES: HIGHS 15–16** A very good time to get new projects up and running; best laid plans go well. **LOWS 1–2; 28–29** Be patient if obstacles stand in your way and these low phases should soon pass.

OCTOBER: MAIN TRENDS: 3–4 You're at your most formidable now – talks go swimmingly and this is an excellent time to take decisive action. **8–9** Entertainment and leisure appeal to you so get your social and romantic life organised. **23–24** Expect to have a high profile and to gain a lot of welcome attention now. **KEY DATES: HIGHS 12–14** A good time to ask a favour of someone close or do something for them. **LOWS 26–27** A short-term low-key period when you may lack effectiveness.

NOVEMBER: MAIN TRENDS: 1–2 Financial dealings may reap rewards and give you an opportunity to appreciate all the good things that life has to offer. **25–26** Planetary influences favour important meetings; what you learn from a colleague can only do you good. **26–27** Consider withdrawing a little from partnerships or group events and take the chance to do your own thing. **KEY DATES: HIGHS 8–10** Keep up a high personal profile now – being at the centre of the action can make you a success. **LOWS 22–24** If you are suffering from a lack of motivation, wind things down a little.

DECEMBER: MAIN TRENDS: 9–10 Trust your instincts to help guide you in the right direction. **12–13** A favourable time for public relations or making new friends; don't be afraid to take the starring role. **22–23** A stable and positive time, but one in which you work best alone. This might help your personal goals. **KEY DATES: HIGHS 6–7** Trends boost your personal self-confidence, which should, in turn, help your ambitions. **LOWS 19–21** Progress may be limited during this sluggish phase.

Michael McIntyre

© PA Images

In 2004, following another year of being ignored at the Edinburgh Festival, Michael Mcintyre wept as he sat in a café, describing the situation as 'hell on earth'. Just this one anecdote speaks volumes about his character, and his powerful need to succeed. Michael's swift rise from obscurity to household name following his first Royal Variety Performance in 2006 has seen him go from strength to strength with shows including *Live at the Apollo* and *Comedy Roadshow*. Of course, he couldn't do it without the huge fan base who clearly adore him. He's said to be Britain's highest-paid comedian. How so?

The answer is hard graft and that iron-will to succeed – both qualities that are found on his birth chart. Michael Hazen James Mcintyre was born on 21 February 1976 at 5.34 pm in Merton, UK, which gives him industrious Virgo rising, Sun in sensitive Pisces and Moon in passionate Scorpio. This combination (Virgo with Scorpio) is unstoppable once it decides on a goal. There's grit and emotional determination and a cool, calculating edge. A Mars (energy) contact with Neptune (spirituality) helps him tune into people and the prevailing mood and he uses this to hold a mirror up to everyday concerns and find humour in the absurdity of day-to-day life. With Moon in Scorpio Michael's very emotional, but he won't suffer fools gladly and is ready to play 'hardball' when needs be. He once walked offstage after someone in the front row used their phone during a concert!

It's a cliché that comedians become comedians because they want to be loved, but this sentiment might apply to Michael. With Venus's harsh alignment with taskmaster Saturn he secretly fears he isn't worthy of the love and admiration of his fans. This makes him work doubly hard, and Jupiter aspecting Saturn signifies the ambition, and hard knocks from which he's emerged with good survival skills. The Saturn placement is the real key to Michael's character, as he's vulnerable and sensitive in ways other people aren't and success is crucial to him. It drives him to overcome his fears.

Taskmaster Saturn has given Michael many hard lessons in recent years, but now lucky and opportunistic Jupiter brings the reward. This trend will continue into 2019 with new social opportunities in the middle of the year. In March and June there may be opportunities to seize the day with an unexpected, lucrative career offer. However, personal and domestic life is where all the focus is this year. Deeply attached to the home, he may be feeling unsettled this year as issues from the past assume significance. There may also be a plan to move to a bigger house. Happily, the indications are that any change will turn out for the best in the long run.

19

TAURUS BORN PEOPLE

Birthdays: 21 April to 21 May inclusive
Planet: Venus. Birthstone: Emerald. Lucky day: Friday

Keynote for the Year: *This should be one of your best years for joining forces with someone, either in business or in love. You may find it harder to widen your horizons, however.*

JANUARY: MAIN TRENDS: 1–2 Your social life should provide some light relief from any current pressures and a romantic encounter may go the way you would like. **5–6** Trends make you high profile and should see you getting out and about in the world. Make the best of professional opportunities. **20–21** Communication improves as your mind gets sharper; you should be able to win an argument, especially one that really matters. **KEY DATES: HIGHS 15–16** A good time to get things done so get an early start. **LOWS 27–29** Present trends undermine any desire to get ahead and accomplish tasks quickly, so take it easy.

FEBRUARY: MAIN TRENDS: 3–4 Domestic matters bring you joy and you enjoy entertaining so why not invite friends over? **9–10** You may now feel that the sun shines only for you; you are centre of attention and not afraid to use this to your advantage. **18–19** The planets put the focus on your interaction with others. In particular, a romantic occasion may bring out your best side and it should be easy to get your own way. **KEY DATES: HIGHS 11–12** Your luckiest days of the month, and a planetary shift also enhances your powers of attraction. **LOWS 24–25** Prepare for some frustrations on the road ahead, possibly born of oversights. Check and double-check everything now.

MARCH: MAIN TRENDS: 1–3 You may feel you are at a crossroads with some serious decisions to make. It may help if you simplify things at work if you can. **20–21** You have a natural flair for working with others and your powers of diplomacy are at their strongest. **26–27** Get organised and improve your efficiency at work. There may also be lots of useful things to do with regard to a new project. **KEY DATES: HIGHS 10–12** Recognise your opportunities, seize them with both hands and this could be a profitable time. **LOWS 23–24** Accept that you have to cope with day-to-day problems and don't allow a lack of confidence to lead you to avoid your responsibilities.

APRIL: MAIN TRENDS: 16–17 Rid yourself of something that's not really working out as planned, especially if things come to boiling point. **18–19** Social activities may revolve around the home and family – a great period for domestic improvements and nostalgic journeys. **22–23** Use your communication skills to help you maintain connections and keep in touch with others; this is a powerful factor in any success. **KEY DATES: HIGHS 7–8** With a bit of positive thinking there's lots you can do to further the cause of progress right now. **LOWS 20–21** Beware of pitfalls and prioritise carefully – then stick to your guns!

MAY: MAIN TRENDS: 6–7 Capitalise on opportunities in your career now, especially if you receive support, or even a favour, from your superiors. **15–16** A good time to pursue new relationships. If you are already in a relationship, you should get a clear sense of your partner's feelings towards you. **20–21** 'Never a dull moment' is the motto now, especially with regard to group events. Acquaintances could emerge from the woodwork just at the right time. **KEY DATES: HIGHS 4–5; 31** Big decisions might turn out better than expected. **LOWS 17–18** Just when you thought nothing could go wrong – boom! In these circumstances, take a cautious approach to decision making.

JUNE: MAIN TRENDS: 4–5 Love life and romance is your best area, and you have what it takes to make your social life happy and stimulating. **9–10** Use your heightened intuition to improve your skill and efficiency and be open to innovative ideas. **21–22** Your instincts are at their sharpest right now, making this a great time to get involved with any form of research or investigation. **KEY DATES: HIGHS 1; 28–29** If you get the 'green light' in a big project it's time to get a move on! **LOWS 13–14** Expect to have to overcome certain obstacles, perhaps relating to significant information that you fail to receive.

JULY: MAIN TRENDS: 3–4 Take the chance to travel if you can and, if it appeals to you, why not opt for a little culture? **23–24** You should be making good strides in your career and a few rewards might come your way. This is also a good time to get a personal problem into perspective. **28–29** A beneficial period for teamwork when there may some good ideas in the air – stay tuned, you never know what you'll learn! **KEY DATES: HIGHS 25–26** Lady Luck is on your side so set time aside for your favourite pastimes. **LOWS 10–11** Put aside big decisions for now, as this is not the luckiest part of the month.

AUGUST: MAIN TRENDS: 11–12 Trends favour your professional life; specifically, a problem at work may come to a successful conclusion. **19–20** Impressive and assured in the limelight now, social events are improved by your presence. **24–25** The challenge may be to prioritise and eschew other interests; this will be worthwhile during this crucial period of renewal in your life. **KEY DATES: HIGHS 21–23** If you are prepared to take a risk, the results may delight you during this lucky period. **LOWS 7–8** Setbacks may get you down so get plenty of rest until this phase passes.

SEPTEMBER: MAIN TRENDS: 13–14 Favourable influences govern your social activities – friends old and new alike could play a very significant role in your life. **15–16** Romance is high on your agenda, as is making new acquaintances. Your popularity enables you to get others to say 'yes' to anything. **23–24** A rewarding phase when everything conspires to bring out the best in you where close personal relationships are concerned. **KEY DATES: HIGHS 17–19** Your self-determination may help you to get your own way. Trends also favour taking a little measured chance, although always heed your instincts. **LOWS 3–4; 30** Err on the side of caution at work today, Taurus!

OCTOBER: MAIN TRENDS: 3–4 Trends suggest that appointments and meetings may have to be rescheduled so prepare for this by having a back-up plan. **8–9** Life should be easy, especially if you get out and about and blow the cobwebs away. **23–24** Teamwork is positively highlighted in your chart; you should be able to get the most from colleagues and friends. **KEY DATES: HIGHS 15–16** Speed ahead of the competition with a little assistance from Lady Luck. **LOWS 28–29** Keep your demands of others to a minimum and ambitions on the back burner during this low period.

NOVEMBER: MAIN TRENDS: 1–2 Dealings with those in authority, especially at work, look set to do you some favours – but don't be hurried into making a major decision. **22–23** Your intuition will serve you well if a professional plan hangs in the balance. **26–27** Take your partner's feelings into account if you run into some conflict. Consideration will help you overcome a problem. **KEY DATES: HIGHS 11–12** Make use of your energy to get ahead with important projects and they should be a success. **LOWS 24–25** Don't be afraid to cancel social engagements if you feel that quiet time at home is what you need.

DECEMBER: MAIN TRENDS: 6–7 Trends assist you to get the best at work or in practical matters and you should see some tangible progress from your efforts. **20–21** Don't be surprised if you see some financial improvements. Build on recent fresh starts and make the most of them. **24–25** Vital news may come your way and give you the edge in debates or topical discussion. **KEY DATES: HIGHS 8–10** A lucky time, and one to get ahead and make tracks. **LOWS 22–23** Don't take on too many or too varied responsibilities now – a personal issue may set you back and give you pause for thought.

GEMINI BORN PEOPLE
Birthdays: 22 May to 21 June inclusive
Planet: Mercury. Birthstone: Agate. Lucky day: Wednesday

Keynote for the Year: *A fortunate influence governs your personal relationships. The actions of others may be lucky for you this year, but you must pay careful attention to joint financial or business matters.*

JANUARY: MAIN TRENDS: 4–5 Life may now contain more than a few pleasant moments; short journeys and conversations especially can make life sweet. **7–8** Get out and explore new interests as the need for freedom of movement may lead to something scintillating. **20–21** Though you have sharp insight into the workings of others, you may be under unexpected pressure to adapt your position. **KEY DATES: HIGHS 17–18** There may be opportunities for expansion at work but any practical decision should work out well. **LOWS 2–4; 30–31** You won't be a winner during these planetary low periods so get plenty of rest and recharge your batteries.

FEBRUARY: MAIN TRENDS: 3–4 Trends highlight your career and it seems that you will benefit from some help and enjoy a good working atmosphere. **10–11** You'd benefit from taking a break but if this isn't an option, vary your daily schedule as much as possible. Anything that broadens your horizons is positively highlighted. **18–19** All domestic matters are reassuring and fulfilling so spend time at home if you can. **KEY DATES: HIGHS 13–15** A very advantageous phase career wise – get your ideas across to your superiors. **LOWS 26–27** Keep your expectations of life simple and put ambitions on the back burner.

MARCH: MAIN TRENDS: 1–3 You may prefer the company of your friends over your partner right now but if you see this as just some space for yourself it needn't be a bad thing. **20–21** Don't be afraid of your desire to retreat from the world right now, this is no bad thing. Ponder your next move and assess your progress so far. **28–29** Financially this may prove quite a stable period, cushioning you while you make forward plans. This is where your strengths lie. **KEY DATES: HIGHS 13–14** Minor changes may make your goals more achievable, especially in professional endeavours. **LOWS 25–27** Prepare to suffer a few delays. Your dealings with others may be more trouble than they're worth!

APRIL: MAIN TRENDS: 17–18 New information and ideas may enhance your life and others support your views – a great day, all in all. **20–21** A happy-go-lucky period for romance, don't be afraid to act with confidence and take the lead. **24–25** With bags of energy and, better still, a little luck this is a high point when you should aim straight for your targets. **KEY DATES: HIGHS 9–10** You can successfully handle several different jobs right now so keep your options open. **LOWS 22–23** You may lack inspiration so this is not the most favourable time to make important plans, take some time out instead.

MAY: MAIN TRENDS: 8–9 Certain plans may now come to fruition as issues to do with finance and property are looking good; actually, the results may prove better than expected. **15–16** Your intuitive, quick responses help with problem solving and may tune into what other people are thinking. **22–23** Communication with co-workers and bosses alike may be beneficial. Also, a good time to think seriously about a plan. **KEY DATES: HIGHS 6–7** Trends give you the confidence to carry off even the most audacious actions! **LOWS 19–20** Stick to the tried-and-tested on these dates and avoid any risks.

JUNE: MAIN TRENDS: 5–6 A favourable time for joint financial dealings – in short, getting the kind of monetary assistance you need from others may be easier than usual. **9–10** The opportunities for professional gain should now be considerable during this high-profile period in which you can steam ahead to success. **21–22** Certain tensions between you and a partner or loved one may increase because of a difference of opinion. A cautious approach may be needed. **KEY DATES: HIGHS 2–4; 30** With your energy at a peak, you should make a success of new interests. Lady Luck is on your side, too. **LOWS 15–17** There may be the odd minor let down now so stick with what you know best.

JULY: MAIN TRENDS: 3–4 In a cheerful, fun-loving and optimistic mood you should attract a lot of attention. Also a period to focus your energies on creative matters. **23–24** A personal situation may be frustrating but becoming over-emotional is not the solution. Keep a cool head and tackle things logically. **29–30** Put your creative ideas to practical use right now. This is also a time of greater independence so make room for fun and personal freedom. **KEY DATES: HIGHS 1; 27–28** Achieving your current objectives may be easy if you just go with the flow. **LOWS 13–14** Potentially, a minor slump; attend to simple tasks and don't complicate matters by trying too hard.

AUGUST: MAIN TRENDS: 11–12 Where competitive matters are concerned, you may find you're out in front as trends aid your potential for success. **21–22** Although you are energetic at work some interactions could prove tense and you're better suited to working alone. Take particular care around those in authority. **26–27** New ideas fall into place and this is now the perfect time to put new plans into operation and get them up and running successfully. **KEY DATES: HIGHS 24–25** Put your present enterprising mood to some material use, at home or at work. **LOWS 9–10** Your ability to influence the course of events seems to be rather limited – take some time to get your strength back.

SEPTEMBER: MAIN TRENDS: 13–14 Your natural curiosity leads you to explore your environment, especially in search of things of cultural influence. **15–16** Seek an outlet for your energy by staying on the move. Travel arrangements made now should turn out very well indeed. **23–24** You may be caught up in a fairly hectic period – refuse to take on any new responsibilities until your outstanding ones are cleared up. **KEY DATES: HIGHS 20–21** You should now be in the driving seat when it comes to achieving your ambitions. Hit the accelerator! **LOWS 5–6** Avoid any tendency towards defeatism in the face of obstacles and go easy on yourself.

OCTOBER: MAIN TRENDS: 5–6 You are set for success so be open to exciting new opportunities at this time of dynamic action and energy. **8–9** A harmonious time, especially for family matters; those around you are supportive. **23–24** Unexpected disruptions might give you a headache but this is still a favourable time to cut back and get rid of clutter. **KEY DATES: HIGHS 17–18** The best time of the month to make a fresh start; personal advantages may be the result. **LOWS 2–4; 30–31** Take time for recuperation to regain your strength.

NOVEMBER: MAIN TRENDS: 1–2 Money, property and possessions and how better to acquire them may be top of your agenda at this key time in the month. **22–23** A change for the better may lie in your love life so romantically you should take the lead. You may get some social opportunities, too. **26–27** Trends favour financial ventures so look for opportunities in this area, but always take advice before you act. **KEY DATES: HIGHS 13–15** All things are possible under this influence and the help of friends is most useful. **LOWS 26–27** A 'shot in the dark' right now could well miss by a mile – this is not your luckiest time.

DECEMBER: MAIN TRENDS: 9–10 Rewarding times on the social scene and you have little trouble finding yourself among the right company and making friends. **20–21** Social and romantic trends continue to be highlighted. You may also get some approval from associates or colleagues. **22–23** Professional developments get a boost so make sure you are in the best position to maximise any opportunity. **KEY DATES: HIGHS 11–12** Naturally adaptable, you take even major changes in your stride. **LOWS 24–25** Don't be over-dependent on luck or the good will of others.

CANCER BORN PEOPLE
Birthdays: 22 June to 22 July inclusive
Planet: Moon. Birthstone: Ruby. Lucky day: Monday

Keynote for the Year: *Personal one-to-one relationships may bring serious responsibilities this year as certain matters come to a head. Work-wise, be open to change – good things are in store!*

JANUARY: MAIN TRENDS: 1–2 Knowledge and understanding are strong motivators now and a hidden truth may surface. Others may be open to your suggestions. **5–6** You may experience a snag as your career direction (and path to success) clashes with personal interests. A time to seek balance. **21–22** Developments in your job may be difficult but solutions may be found if you remain calm. **KEY DATES: HIGHS 19–20** Use your sound intuition and judgement to put new ideas into action. **LOWS 5–6** Your power may be rather thin on the ground and your persuasive skills limited so don't act on any rash impulses.

FEBRUARY: MAIN TRENDS: 3–4 Fulfilment may come from broadening your horizons and being open to new experiences. Welcome any opportunity to do something stimulating or cultural. **10–11** Self-sacrifice and giving to others may be more rewarding than personal gain. **18–19** If the pursuit of your personal objectives and ambitions leads to setbacks and defeat, try to keep a sense of perspective. **KEY DATES: HIGHS 16–17** Make use of this trend to double your luck, as you should have a great deal of control over day-to-day matters. **LOWS 1–2; 28** Don't take on too many duties during this time of limited strength.

MARCH: MAIN TRENDS: 3–4 A great time for pioneering action and to throw yourself into improving life. You thrive in any situation where you're in the driving seat. **20–21** Be practical and methodical, doing important things only; business dealings may need handling with diplomacy. **26–27** New situations may go against the grain and you may need to decide whether any risk is worth the change they bring. **KEY DATES: HIGHS 15–16** Your potential for successful progress is strong under this lucky trend for Cancer. **LOWS 1–2; 28–29** Keep things simple and pay particular attention to your private life.

APRIL: MAIN TRENDS: 17–18 This influence boosts all matters of communication so talks and discussions have much to offer and may turn out very well indeed. **20–21** A pleasant, light-hearted influence when communication continues to improve on all levels. You now feel comfortably in the mainstream of life. **22–23** Get an early start, be creative and let the world know who you are; if you capitalise on these trends you should find personal fulfilment. **KEY DATES: HIGHS 11–12** Take action to expand your professional endeavours and you may pick up some valuable information. **LOWS 24–25** Maintain a low profile, attend to unfinished tasks and get plenty of rest.

MAY: MAIN TRENDS: 6–7 A reflective phase when you may look within yourself. You can revive your spirits with some quiet meditation. **15–16** Current planetary trends suggest an optimistic air and a thirst to explore new ideas. Seek out those on a similar mental or spiritual wavelength. **19–20** Some daily obstacles may be unavoidable, and where major tasks are at stake a go-slow policy could be best. **KEY DATES: HIGHS 8–9** Be confident and self-assured and, in turn, others may prove generous and supportive of your ideas. **LOWS 21–23** Don't expect a smooth passage through life now, but at the same time don't be beaten too easily!

JUNE: MAIN TRENDS: 3–4 Get out and about under this optimistic trend for inspirational ideas; your readiness to learn should make you very attractive. **9–10** Trends highlight the sphere of love and romance, which should put you in the mood to get out and enjoy some time with your partner. **21–22**

Your ego is high, especially when it comes to your ambitions, but be sure to keep your expectations on a realistic basis. **KEY DATES: HIGHS 5–6** Take any opportunity to get ahead and test how far your luck runs. **LOWS 18–19** Some minor complications at work or at home are likely. Try not to get the wrong end of the stick.

JULY: MAIN TRENDS: 4–5 Optimism and a willingness to take one day at a time is what will get you through now – avoid focusing on the negative and put your considerable creativity to good use. **23–24** Money-making may be that much easier and more profitable now, and you should feel nicely secure. **28–29** You will do best in situations that allow you to use your social skills and organise something universally popular. **KEY DATES: HIGHS 2–3; 29–31** A great time to put new plans into practice – you may even have a card up your sleeve that you can use in negotiations. **LOWS 15–16** Setbacks may be unavoidable so postpone big tasks if possible.

AUGUST: MAIN TRENDS: 13–14 Your personal influence and effectiveness may help you to consolidate your financial position; a favourable period for cautious investments. **21–22** A secure period when you should make steady progress towards your career goals. Have confidence in yourself. **23–24** People on whom you generally rely may prove anything but reliable now, and loved ones or colleagues may have different views on a personal matter, too. **KEY DATES: HIGHS 26–27** A bit of faith in yourself should work miracles when it comes to getting your own way. **LOWS 11–12** Don't worry too much about keeping up with everyone else and work at your own pace.

SEPTEMBER: MAIN TRENDS: 13–14 You're at your most convincing and persuasive in social relationships making this an excellent time for clear-headed discussions. **15–16** Your acquisitive side comes to the fore. Remember whilst you are gunning for material things to avoid possessive behaviour with friends and partners. **24–25** Trends now reduce any pressure on you and help things run smoothly. Travel related to your career is particularly highlighted. **KEY DATES: HIGHS 22–23** This is your time of the month, Cancer, so whatever the plan is, take the lead and go for it! **LOWS 7–9** You may feel on a temporary downer so take things slowly and get a couple of early nights.

OCTOBER: MAIN TRENDS: 3–4 Nostalgia has come calling and this is a great time for reliving the past. Trends affecting your home life may lead you to some interesting food for thought. **8–9** Look ahead to a period of high creative fulfilment. Also, relationships may prove good for your ego. **23–24** Your love life is favourable and when it comes to your social life you know how to please others and enlist some co-operation. **KEY DATES: HIGHS 20–21** Take a few chances to get ahead of the pack. **LOWS 5–7** Don't allow a hectic phase at home to distract you from concerns out in the wider world.

NOVEMBER: MAIN TRENDS: 3–4 You may have all the help you need to find a new way to get ahead at work. **22–23** Your social or romantic life may be satisfying, with many good times to be had. **26–27** Trends suggest that a charming newcomer may present you with a social opportunity. You are attractive to others and feel the need for freedom, so go for it. **KEY DATES: HIGHS 16–17** Potentially, your luckiest time of the month when material and emotional good things look set to come your way. **LOWS 1–2; 29–30** Keep your objectives within easy reach but don't allow your professional plans to be thwarted.

DECEMBER: MAIN TRENDS: 9–10 A breezy period in relationships when co-operation and give and take are the key phrases. Long-term attachments may become a little more interesting! **20–21** A time of transition when you may want to renew certain aspects of your life and cut out the deadwood. **22–23** Trends suggest that certain practical matters can be taken for granted and need far less work than you thought. **KEY DATES: HIGHS 13–14** A lucky phase and a great time to make an impression on others. **LOWS 26–27** Don't worry if you lack the enthusiasm to get on with things now, there will be time later.

200-year Perpetual Calendar

Do you know on which day of the week you or your friends were born? You may remember that World War II was declared on Sunday, 3 September 1939, but on which day did World War I start?

This calendar, created originally by C. E. Forsythe, allows you to find the weekday for any date from 1850 to 2050. You will find it useful and informative and very simple to use. Just follow the instructions to check birthdays, events and special occasions.

- Find the year in Table A.
- Follow across on the same line to Table B and select the number under the relevant month.
- Add this number to the date.
- Look up this number in Table C and follow across to the left to find the day of the week.

Table A / **Table B**

								Jan	Feb	Mar	Apri	May	June	July	Aug	Sept	Oct	Nov	Dec
	1850	1878		1918	1946	1974	2002	2030	2	5	5	1	3	6	1	4	0	2	5	0
	1851	1879		1919	1947	1975	2003	2031	3	6	6	2	4	0	2	5	1	3	6	1
*	1852	1880		1920	1848	1976	2004	2032	4	0	1	4	6	2	4	0	3	5	1	3
	1853	1881		1921	1949	1977	2005	2033	6	2	2	5	0	3	5	1	4	6	2	4
	1854	1882		1922	1950	1978	2006	2034	0	3	3	6	1	4	6	2	5	0	3	5
	1855	1883		1923	1951	1979	2007	2035	1	4	4	0	2	5	0	3	6	1	4	6
*	1856	1884		1924	1952	1980	2008	2036	2	5	6	2	4	0	2	5	1	3	6	1
	1857	1885		1925	1953	1981	2009	2037	4	0	0	3	5	1	3	6	2	4	0	2
	1858	1886		1926	1954	1982	2010	2038	5	1	1	4	6	2	4	0	3	5	1	3
	1859	1887		1927	1955	1983	2011	2039	6	2	2	5	0	3	5	1	4	6	2	4
*	1860	1888		1928	1956	1984	2012	2040	0	3	4	0	2	5	0	3	6	1	4	6
	1861	1889	1901	1929	1957	1985	2013	2041	2	5	5	1	3	6	1	4	0	2	5	0
	1862	1890	1902	1930	1958	1986	2014	2042	3	6	6	2	4	0	2	5	1	3	6	1
	1863	1891	1903	1931	1959	1987	2015	2043	4	0	0	3	5	1	3	6	2	4	0	2
*	1864	1892	1904	1932	1960	1988	2016	2044	5	1	2	5	0	3	5	1	4	6	2	4
	1865	1893	1905	1933	1961	1989	2017	2045	0	3	3	6	1	4	6	2	5	0	3	5
	1866	1894	1906	1934	1962	1990	2018	2046	1	4	4	0	2	5	0	3	6	1	4	6
	1867	1895	1907	1935	1963	1991	2019	2047	2	5	5	1	3	6	1	4	0	2	5	0
*	1868	1896	1908	1936	1964	1992	2020	2048	3	6	0	3	5	1	3	6	2	4	0	2
	1869	1897	1909	1937	1965	1993	2021	2049	5	1	1	4	6	2	4	0	3	5	1	3
	1870	1898	1910	1938	1966	1994	2022	2050	6	2	2	5	0	3	5	1	4	6	2	4
	1871	1899	1911	1939	1967	1995	2023		0	3	3	6	1	4	6	2	5	0	3	5
*	1872		1912	1940	1968	1996	2024		1	4	5	1	3	6	1	4	0	2	5	0
	1873		1913	1941	1969	1997	2025		3	6	6	2	4	0	2	5	1	3	6	1
	1874		1914	1942	1970	1998	2026		4	0	0	3	5	1	3	6	2	4	0	2
	1875		1915	1943	1971	1999	2027		5	1	1	4	6	2	4	0	3	5	1	3
*	1876		1916	1944	1972	2000	2028		6	2	3	6	1	4	6	2	5	0	3	5
	1877	1900	1917	1945	1973	2001	2029		1	4	4	0	2	5	0	3	6	1	4	6

Table C

Sunday	1	8	15	22	29	36
Monday	2	9	16	23	30	37
Tuesday	3	10	17	24	31	
Wednesday	4	11	18	25	32	
Thursday	5	12	19	26	33	
Friday	6	13	20	27	34	
Saturday	7	14	21	28	35	

Example: 3 March 1896
March 1896 = 0
Date = 3
0 + 3 = 3 so it fell on a Tuesday

Example: 27 July 2005
July 2005 = 5
Date = 27
5 + 27 = 32 so it will fall on a Wednesday

* Years on the lines to the right of the asterisks are leap years.

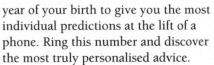

27

Personal Signs in Chinese Astrology

In Chinese astrology, your character type is defined by the year of your birth. Each year is associated with one of 12 animals. The cycle of animals repeats in the sequence listed below, beginning with the rat. Years of the rat are 1948, 1960, 1972 and so on. The Ox is therefore 1949, 1961 and so on, or you can search online for your sign. For January/February birthdays, check online when Chinese new year fell in your year – if it was after your birthday, your sign will be the one of the year before.

RAT: Clever and resourceful, the rat is the charmer, intelligent, practical and quick-witted. Social types, they make loyal friends, but can be opinionated and a little cunning at times.

OX: Reserved, practical and inflexible. Meticulous planners, they don't put up with nonsense and can be stubborn, although they can be relied on for practical skills, common sense and strength of purpose.

TIGER: Unpredictable and with a fierce love of freedom, the tiger has a natural magnetism and strong independent streak. Creative and tireless, tigers are apt to change their minds.

RABBIT: Don't be fooled by the mild-mannered and home-loving rabbit, there's a manipulative streak and a desire to succeed which can push you out of the way if they can't diplomatically bring you round to their point of view. A great sensualist, but not always good under pressure.

DRAGON: The dragon represents a positive, life-enhancing strength, sometimes impulsive, always energetic and assertive. Perhaps not the most patient person you'll ever meet, if there's a negative side, it's their tendency to be self-opinionated and an inability to apologise!

SNAKE: Snakes are essentially reserved creatures. Elegant, charming, kind and sensual, they make loyal friends, but there's a part that very few get to know. Highly astute, it's hard to get the better of them, nor a good idea to make enemies of them, as they could strike when you least expect it.

HORSE: An exuberant nature and quick brain characterise this natural actor and perfect salesperson. Always interesting, with an eccentric and ingenious streak, they have a great sense of fun, although they don't always know what they are talking about and can be cantankerous if crossed.

GOAT: Refined, soft-hearted and intellectual, these people tend to be sensual and sometimes extravagant, although they can be insecure and use a natural reserve to protect them from what they see as a threatening world. Don't upset them, as they have a long memory.

MONKEY: Always active, sexy and versatile, these can be the know-it-alls if they get all their own way, but criticism can wound their over-size ego. They relish a challenge, and are more than capable of sorting out most problems quickly and efficiently.

ROOSTER: Sometimes fussy and fastidious, but with an amazing capacity for accuracy, these people speak their minds, have unbounded curiosity, and are reliable and trustworthy. Very tidy-minded, they won't put up with other people's mess – literal or otherwise.

DOG: Communicative and excitable, this is a mercurial character, usually optimistic but inclined to be negative if things start to go wrong. Charming, hard-working and affectionate, they are likeable characters who make good friends, but are best not cornered.

PIG: Hard-working and shy, these sensual people respond well to attention. Although it is not easy to understand them, they make true friends. Stubborn, once committed, they rarely lose a battle.

THE ELEMENTS: Each year is associated with an element as well as with an animal, which further defines your characteristics. The elements change every two years, so 1952 and 1953 are water years, 1954 and 1955 are wood years, and so on. You can find the element for your year on-line. Water people are creative, compassionate, kind and understanding. Wood people are warm, considerate, generous and co-operative. Fire people are dynamic, purposeful and strong. Earth people are patient, hard-working, reliable and sometimes stubborn. Metal people have strength of character and determination.

2019 – Year of the Pig

Chinese astrology works on a slightly different time scale from the more familiar Western branch of the study, and because of this Chinese New Year does not commence in 2019 until 5 February. Until that time, remains under the rulership of the Dog, the influence of which has been felt throughout society for the last twelve months or so. The ancient Chinese scribes identified this period as being one of reasonable peace, with the forces of law and order predominating and moves towards peace being the norm.

However, from 5 February the influence changes somewhat as the year of the Pig dawns. Often thought of as being similar to the Western zodiac sign of Scorpio, Pig years are times when things are more likely to happen, and often in an unpredictable or even violent way. During Pig years, diplomacy on the world stage sometimes takes a back seat and people tend to take the law into their own hands. However the Pig is very idealistic, so we should see a year during which people all over the world will be more than willing to stand up for what they believe, even bringing down governments if they consider that their rights are being abused. Pig years are times of gains and losses and periods when common sense is sometimes thrown out of the window in the heat of emotionally motivated events.

The element associated with the Pig in 2019 is Earth. This pairing tends to take some of the edge off the unpredictable and somewhat volatile nature of the Pig, making people less aggressive and instead influencing them to centre their ambitions around realistic targets. Earth Pigs are known to enjoy conversation, especially verbal sparring, and are usually popular amongst their friends. They are patient, and are always punctual, believing lateness to be bad manners. Governments of countries and states around the world will also be more likely to show patience with regard to their neighbours and violent clashes might be avoided as a result.

If you were born under the year of the Pig, roughly after the start of February in the years 1935, 1947, 1959, 1971, 1983, 1995 or 2007, you are likely to be passionate, deep, sexy and very much inclined to fire from the hip. You are an idealist and will do almost anything to make sure your opinions are heard. You are also a deeply loyal character who would move mountains for your friends. You love deeply but you can also bear a grudge for years if you feel particularly slighted, and like the elephant you never forget. Pigs are extremely hard-working personalities and are never afraid to go the extra mile to achieve their ambitions. Once a Pig has set their heart on a particular object of their affections, they will go all out to make sure they get it.

In Chinese culture the pig is seen as a lazy animal and so people born under this sign are sometimes perceived as sharing those characteristics, although this is rarely the case. Pigs might be easygoing, but they are also brave and often well-educated. You could do far worse than to have a Pig on your side!

LEO BORN PEOPLE

Birthdays: 23 July to 23 August inclusive
Planet: Sun. Birthstone: Sapphire. Lucky day: Sunday

Keynote for the Year: *A fun year for your love life when new plans can be initiated with relative ease. A more serious element may prevail at work, with some challenges to overcome.*

JANUARY: MAIN TRENDS: 1–2 Your social life gets a boost even this early in the new year, and you enjoy the company of like-minded people. **5–6** Some new romantic opportunities may be in store for some Leos, while those in long-term relationships should be enjoying a sweet and happy atmosphere. **19–20** Put your impressive personality to use and go for what you want right now – this approach should ensure successful results. **KEY DATES: HIGHS 21–22** Trends assist you to overcome any setbacks at home or at work. **LOWS 7–9** Prepare to have to contend with unexpected obstacles; your pace seems to be sluggish, at best.

FEBRUARY: MAIN TRENDS: 2–3 Your forte lies in your friendliness and sociability right now – you would make a good diplomat or negotiator. A partner may play an important role in your career. **10–11** Give in to your strong sense of wanderlust now as trends suggest you may encounter something stimulating. **20–21** The planets help you to find an efficient way to side-step obstacles – on time too! **KEY DATES: HIGHS 18–19** Leo is the sign of the moment so set your sights on beating the competition. **LOWS 4–5** Don't allow disappointments to bring you down, especially if important engagements have to be broken.

MARCH: MAIN TRENDS: 1–3 Relationships can be complicated and troublesome now so you may benefit from spending some time alone. **20–21** A new sparkle may be evident in your social life as you broaden your horizons and learn something new about the world. **26–27** If you let someone down you will take it as a personal failure, but remember that no one can please all the people all the time. **KEY DATES: HIGHS 17–18** Your enthusiasm for life may be very apparent and you won't be slow in taking advantage of it. **LOWS 3–4; 30–31** Prepare for some minor delays at work and don't be too hard on yourself if things go awry.

APRIL: MAIN TRENDS: 17–18 You may get the chance to improve some aspects of your life – follow your intuition and trust your instincts. **20–21** The social atmosphere at work should be happy and agreeable, but don't let this hinder industrious work and thoughts of your ambitions. **22–23** Focus on personal relationships and friendships now; trends favour all partnerships whether business or pleasure. **KEY DATES: HIGHS 13–14** A time of noteworthy personal effectiveness, stronger than you might have imagined. **LOWS 1; 26–27** Put off making important decisions and attend to smaller, everyday matters instead.

MAY: MAIN TRENDS: 6–7 There may be more money, and emotional support, available for new projects than you had expected. **15–16** You throw your energies into dynamic thinking and you may well learn something new and useful as a result. **20–21** Things may not be plain sailing at work or in practical matters; take care not to overstep the mark with people in authority. **KEY DATES: HIGHS 11–12** Personal and professional aims should now be easily attainable as you find others are on your side. **LOWS 24–25** Beware that if you're in too much of a hurry to achieve your objectives, your progress may get stuck in a lower gear.

JUNE: MAIN TRENDS: 4–5 Expect one or two ups and downs, but don't be afraid to get rid of whatever isn't working for you right now. **9–10** Home is now the best place to be. A good time to invite friends or family over. **22–23** So much is now geared towards making your personal life more efficient you may have to jettison something from other areas of your life. **KEY DATES: HIGHS 7–8** Trends favourably influence the workplace, making this a great period to make changes professionally. **LOWS 20–21** Lacking motivation as you are now, risky ventures are probably best left alone.

JULY: MAIN TRENDS: 2–3 A high spot in the month when you may be able to attract new romantic interests – it may be time to celebrate! **23–24** You may have some good ideas for improvements to a daily routine, even if this does involve getting rid of something. **28–29** Trends favour money matters but you may need to use your charm to get plans and pet projects running the way you would like. **KEY DATES: HIGHS 4–5** The 'green light' for go is on so make the most of professional or personal advantages. **LOWS 17–19** Play it safe if you need to make important decisions especially at work, and make time for relaxation.

AUGUST: MAIN TRENDS: 11–12 For maximum happiness seek out wide open spaces and don't be talked out of doing something you really want to do. **21–22** Those in positions of authority may be more approachable than usual which could make a tremendous difference to your professional life. **23–24** When it comes to business, a little clever thinking could mean real gains. **KEY DATES: HIGHS 1–2; 28–29** Lady Luck is on your side which could be helpful if you need to take a little gamble on something, not necessarily financial. **LOWS 14–15** Trends indicate a deceptive influence – make sure you don't deceive yourself!

SEPTEMBER: MAIN TRENDS: 13–14 Mentally you are firing on all cylinders and you love a good argument. Take care not to jump to conclusions about others, though. **15–16** Make sure you are not so focused on the big picture that you overlook important details. Trends governing your career look quite rosy. **22–23** Planetary influences bring out your enquiring mind and fascination with trivia. But you can also put your versatility to good use in many areas. **KEY DATES: HIGHS 24–25** Extend yourself, even burn the candle at both ends, during this productive phase. **LOWS 10–11** A plan of action may need to be thought out more carefully or, better still, postponed.

OCTOBER: MAIN TRENDS: 3–4 Your love life could rejuvenate your spirits and a light-hearted, social occasion may bring new people into your life. **5–6** Work-wise this phase may prove rather low key, but personal relationships and being wrapped up in your own little world should be rewarding. **24–25** A certain element of fatigue may prevail so go a little easy on yourself. **KEY DATES: HIGHS 22–23** You can persuade others around to your way of thinking with relative ease, especially if you seek help from influential people. **LOWS 7–9** You may experience a 'stop-start' effect at work as obstacles force you to slow down.

NOVEMBER: MAIN TRENDS: 1–2 Aim high with your personal goals and objectives – there's much to keep you both interested and well informed. **22–23** New assistance may come your way at work during this upbeat phase when you can satisfy nearly all professional demands. **26–27** Set out to broaden your horizons socially with an appeal to old friends and new associates. Gatherings may be highly fulfilling at this time. **KEY DATES: HIGHS 18–19** You should be in the running for a little luck at the very least. **LOWS 3–5** Don't give way to false optimism and keep a sense of perspective at all times.

DECEMBER: MAIN TRENDS: 9–10 You may feel pretty restless now, especially if you feel mired in old routines. Your sense of adventure pushes you to broaden your horizons. **20–21** A time of quiet contemplation; seek solitude, meditate and put some effort into finding 'answers' within your everyday life. This has beneficial effects. **22–23** Positive change can be expected in your relationships. You should enjoy more romance, excitement and pleasure from those close to you. **KEY DATES: HIGHS 15–16** Where personal dreams and schemes are concerned, most objectives should run according to plan. **LOWS 1–2; 28–30** Not the best time to pursue anything risky so keep your expectations realistic.

VIRGO BORN PEOPLE

Birthdays: 24 August to 23 September inclusive
Planet: Mercury. Birthstone: Sardonyx. Lucky day: Wednesday

Keynote for the Year: *Domestic matters receive a significant planetary boost this year and your plans at home should work out well. Don't let this be overshadowed by challenges in your love life.*

JANUARY: MAIN TRENDS: 1–2 Don't believe everything you hear now as your sources of information may be poorly informed. **5–6** Certain relationships may feel like they're more trouble than they're worth. Shy away from social activities for now. **20–21** Your boundless energy may need vigorous exercise to properly channel it. You shouldn't be short of innovative ideas. **KEY DATES: HIGHS 23–24** Some significant information may come your way and a favourable roll of the dice could benefit your personal life. **LOWS 10–11** Take care when you are talking to people that they don't get the wrong end of the stick.

FEBRUARY: MAIN TRENDS: 3–4 You learn quickly under current trends and your communication skills are good – an excellent day to talk over plans and schemes. **10–11** A boost to leisure and pleasure as entertaining experiences come your way and you enjoy the limelight. A chance meeting may lead to a pleasant surprise. **18–19** Your personal influence is strong and your leadership qualities are apparent. A time when Virgoans should get exactly what they want! **KEY DATES: HIGHS 20–21** Elicit the help of people of influence and you may be surprised by your own achievements. **LOWS 6–8** Expect the pace of progress to be slow at work.

MARCH: MAIN TRENDS: 1–3 The pace of life steps up and important news may require a quick response and immediate action. But don't speak rashly before you think. **21–22** With increased versatility you now have the gift of talking your way out of trouble in any personal conflicts. **26–27** Enjoy time spent with those you know well in familiar places, as old memories and nostalgia occupy your thoughts. **KEY DATES: HIGHS 5–7** Put your gut instinct and intuition to good use and things should work out well. **LOWS 19–20** Beware a tendency to overlook some necessary fine details at work.

APRIL: MAIN TRENDS: 17–18 The course of true love should run smooth – relationships are rewarding and you are marvellous company! **20–21** Proper preparation is the key to success and while the competition may be tough, you can deal with it easily with the right attitude. **22–23** With a new resolve in your outlook and spring in your step you can look ahead to a beneficial period professionally. **KEY DATES: HIGHS 15–16** A romantic occasion may help you get the most from life but practical matters won't suffer as you are able to multi-task successfully. **LOWS 2–3; 29–30** A form of communication may be stressful. Don't take any opinions for granted at this time but instead listen carefully.

MAY: MAIN TRENDS: 6–7 Nice things should be happening in your love life and socially you should enjoy some good company. **15–16** Organise and simplify your routines at work to gain better control, and prioritise and get the important things done first. **20–21** Practical matters may be most enjoyable now so any plans on the drawing board may soon get underway. **KEY DATES: HIGHS 13–14** Positive, lucky trends continue and you could get some help from unlikely quarters. **LOWS 26–28** Emotional matters could be a test of strength or there could be a serious delay – only patience will see you through.

JUNE: MAIN TRENDS: 4–5 You thrive on professional competition, and are excellent at achieving short-term goals. You can complete tasks even under great stress. **11–12** You may prefer to keep a lower profile as you work out how best to deal with others. Fulfilment may lie in finding a way to help someone. **21–22** Time to reflect on your life and the direction it has taken. In this introspective mood,

you may be a little more dependent on loved ones. **KEY DATES: HIGHS 9–10** Some good professional ideas combined with a little chance could lead to big success with certain projects. **LOWS 23–24** Keep to the tried and tested path to bypass any pitfalls.

JULY: MAIN TRENDS: 3–4 With lots of opportunity to do the right thing, you should be taking life in your stride – don't be talked out of it! **23–24** Close relationships may be more satisfying than ever and a loved ones actions might benefit you. **28–29** A really excellent trend for your career or for progress in any area – time to put your best foot forward, Virgo. **KEY DATES: HIGHS 6–7** A combination of effort and luck should enable you to make the most of this powerful trend. **LOWS 20–21** You may have to work harder to accomplish your objectives so put certain things on hold if you can.

AUGUST: MAIN TRENDS: 11–12 It could be make or break time in certain areas – do you end things and start afresh or make the best of it? Only you can decide. **21–22** Trends assist you in the world of finance, and you may meet some interesting business contacts. **23–24** A complete change of scenery will do you the world of good, but at the very least put off mundane obligations that can wait until later. **KEY DATES: HIGHS 3–4; 30–31** This is quite simply an excellent time for brand new starts and getting favours done. **LOWS 16–17** You may have to be on guard for setbacks and delays with an important project.

SEPTEMBER: MAIN TRENDS: 13–14 Your powers of enterprise are good so focus on worthwhile goals and objectives – the strength required is at your fingertips. **15–16** Others may see your fun-loving side and the impact you make has never been greater, especially where practical achievements are concerned. **23–24** A hectic pace prevails, to the point where you are too busy. All aspects of communication go well, however, and may be enlightening. **KEY DATES: HIGHS 26–27** A high spot and lucky period across the board. **LOWS 13–14** If things seem unstable, focus on staying on an even keel in the midst of minor ups and downs.

OCTOBER: MAIN TRENDS: 3–4 This trend could see your plans curtailed by those who hold power – while this is frustrating, make sure you recognise certain limitations. **8–9** The planets help you to see clearly where you're going with your plans and just how you are going to accomplish them. **22–23** Whilst personal issues are favoured, you may be distracted by demands from partners who are in need of some care and attention. **KEY DATES: HIGHS 24–25** If you are in need of a favour, ask and you may receive! **LOWS 10–11** If you encounter a slight decline in your fortunes use it as a break in between important activities.

NOVEMBER: MAIN TRENDS: 1–2 You should enjoy harmony in social settings and this is a good time for entertaining at home. **22–23** Social gatherings should keep you happy enough but at work, beware! – you may find various people let you down in some way. **26–27** A time for romance as trends help to ensure a warm reaction from your loved one. Take time to appreciate the pleasurable aspects of life. **KEY DATES: HIGHS 20–21** Approach the business of the day with confidence and a lot will get done without you having to try too hard. **LOWS 6–7** Prepare for a few unexpected setbacks to progress and leave a margin for error.

DECEMBER: MAIN TRENDS: 9–10 Keep in touch with news and views coming your way, you never know what you might learn. A good time for a productive conversation. **20–21** Put new ideas and schemes into operation and expect an easy path towards your objectives. **22–23** You have great energy and confidence but avoid being in too much of a hurry in the workplace. **KEY DATES: HIGHS 17–18** With the help of Lady Luck, you should speed towards your objectives now. **LOWS 3–4; 31** A planetary low point when it's best to keep life as simple and uncomplicated as possible.

Jeremy Corbyn

© PA Images

There is a significant problem when it comes to assessing anything about the future of Labour leader Jeremy Corbyn in an astrological sense. Nobody knows at what time of day he was born and in this chart especially, this presents a real difficulty. We do know that Jeremy was born on 26 May 1949. There is a method in astrology known as rectification, which allows an assessment of the time of birth using previous, known events from a person's life and by using this method Old Moore calculates that Jeremy may have been born at around 8 pm. This would mean that Scorpio was rising at the time of his birth, and that fits very well with what we know of the man.

Corbyn's chart contains four planets in Gemini: the Sun, Mercury, Venus and Uranus. This means he was born to be a communicator, and yet with Gemini so close to the descendant and opposed to Scorpio rising it was inevitable that he would become hero to some and the exact opposite to others.

This chart displays tenacity, significant self-belief and a gritty determination to follow a path nurtured for years. Jeremy Corbyn is no quitter but while he will fight ceaselessly for his political and social ideals, that alone does not necessarily mean he will achieve his ultimate objective of becoming Prime Minister.

The movements and positions of the planet Uranus feature heavily in Corbyn's progressed chart for the next year or so. Uranus is a strange and even revolutionary planet. Its associations in the progressed chart with its position at Jeremy's birth bring restlessness and a desire to leave cares and worries behind. On the other hand Uranus becomes trine to Saturn before the start of 2019, which could indicate a break in a logjam and new opportunities. Meanwhile Neptune and Venus show a tendency for Jeremy to be rather too idealistic for his own good, which could lead to unpopularity and criticism as 2019 begins. Overriding all of this is the threat of betrayal, not from his enemies but rather his supposed friends.

The real worry lies in the natal chart itself. This is a character who will always suffer from public criticism because of the planetary oppositions to Gemini. His greatest problems come not from himself but from those around him. All in all we see a chart depicting monumental struggle and continued adversity. Taking everything into account, *if* the rectified chart details are correct, Old Moore's assessment is that Jeremy Corbyn is unlikely to achieve the highest political position in Great Britain. It's true that Mr Corbyn has surprised people before. He is a revolutionary and does not understand the meaning of failure. But he will have his work cut out!

OBSTACLES

JANUARY

For High Water add 5h 30m for Bristol, 4h 23m for Hull, 0h 43m for Leith; subtract 2h 21m for Dublin, 1h 26m for Greenock, 2h 29m for Liverpool.

D of M	D of W	Festivals, Events and Anniversaries	Sun at London Rises	Sun at London Sets	High Water at London Bridge am	High Water at London Bridge pm	Moon at London Rises	Moon at London Sets	Weather
			h m	h m	h m	h m	h m	h m	
1	Tu	New Year's Day	08:06	16:01	09 34	22 17	03 09	13 22	A mild, cheerful, uneventful start turning suddenly colder with north winds and snow in the north and east, lasting 7–9 days. Gentle spell mid-month will be countered by a cold blast at the close.
2	W	Bank Holiday (Scotland)	08:06	16:02	10 35	23 12	04 20	13 50	
3	Th	Alaska US state 1959	08:05	16:04	11 31	—	05 28	14 22	
4	F	Battle of Reading 871	08:05	16:05	00 02	12 21	06 31	15 00	
5	Sa	Partial solar eclipse (23 34)	08:05	16:06	00 47	13 07	07 28	15 46	
6	Su	Epiphany	08:05	16:07	01 29	13 50	08 17	16 38	
7	M	Distress signal CQD est. 1904	08:04	16:08	02 08	14 30	08 59	17 36	
8	Tu	Saeed Jaffrey b. 1929	08:04	16:10	02 46	15 10	09 33	18 38	
9	W	Duchess of Cambridge b. 1982	08:03	16:11	03 23	15 48	10 01	19 42	
10	Th	Nicholas Culpepper d. 1654	08:03	16:13	03 59	16 25	10 25	20 46	
11	F	Anglo-Zulu war beg. 1879	08:02	16:14	04 36	17 04	10 47	21 52	
12	Sa	Dame Agatha Christie d. 1976	08:01	16:15	05 14	17 45	11 06	22 58	
13	Su	Costa Concordia sinks 2012	08:01	16:17	05 55	18 31	11 25	—	
14	M	Faye Dunaway b. 1941	08:00	16:18	06 42	19 24	11 45	00 05	
15	Tu	Elizabeth I crowned 1559	07:59	16:20	07 37	20 25	12 07	01 14	
16	W	Peter Butterworth d. 1979	07:58	16:21	08 41	21 28	12 33	02 27	
17	Th	Muhammad Ali b. 1942	07:57	16:23	09 47	22 29	13 05	03 41	
18	F	Peter Mayle d. 2018	07:57	16:25	10 50	23 26	13 45	04 56	
19	Sa	Feast of St Wulstan	07:56	16:26	11 49	—	14 37	06 08	
20	Su	First English parliament 1265	07:54	16:28	00 19	12 43	15 42	07 13	
21	M	Total lunar eclipse (05 12)	07:53	16:30	01 09	13 35	16 58	08 07	
22	Tu	Spain cedes Falkland Is 1771	07:52	16:31	01 57	14 25	18 21	08 50	
23	W	Albright Sec. of State 1997	07:51	16:33	02 45	15 14	19 45	09 25	
24	Th	Conscription introduced 1916	07:50	16:35	03 32	16 03	21 08	09 53	
25	F	Burns Night	07:49	16:36	04 20	16 52	22 28	10 18	
26	Sa	Australia Day	07:47	16:38	05 09	17 43	23 45	10 41	
27	Su	Holocaust Memorial Day	07:46	16:40	06 00	18 37	—	11 03	
28	M	Pride and Prejudice pub. 1813	07:45	16:42	06 55	18 37	00 59	11 27	
29	Tu	George III d. 1820	07:43	16:44	07 55	20 37	02 11	11 54	
30	W	Franklin D. Roosevelt b. 1882	07:42	16:45	08 59	21 40	03 20	12 24	
31	Th	Anna Pavlova b. 1885	07:40	16:47	10 04	22 40	04 24	13 00	

MOON'S PHASES JANUARY 2019

		Days	Hours	Mins
●	New Moon	6	01	28
☽	First Quarter	14	06	45
○	Full Moon	21	05	16
☾	Last Quarter	27	21	10

All times on this page are GMT

PREDICTIONS

The New Moon on 6 January is in Capricorn in a harmonious semi-sextile to Neptune. Neptune is in a destabilising square to Jupiter and Uranus is on the seventh cusp at London. This is a moment of deep uncertainty. The financial markets may be booming but smart investors should invest only in safe bets and avoid potential bubbles. In Washington, the American government runs into major obstacles and is engaged in a constitutional struggle over the extent of its powers. The lunar eclipse passes over Beijing pointing to popular protests against the regime. China's western provinces may be in open revolt. General earthquake alerts will be made in the north-east USA and British Columbia. Flood warnings will be issued in eastern Australia.

The Full Moon on 21 January in Leo is an eclipse on the eighth cusp at London, confirming indications of financial volatility. The housing market looks particularly explosive with sharp rises in parts of the country provoking predictions of a crash. However, the national mood is optimistic, with opinion polls indicating confidence in the future. China is in a warlike mood, sabre-rattling in the South China Sea and launching a series of confrontations with its neighbours through the year.

A firm favourite should win at Cheltenham in the *New Year Meeting*. A 9-year-old may be victorious at the *Clarence House Chase*.

FEBRUARY

For High Water add 5h 30m for Bristol, 4h 23m for Hull, 0h 43m for Leith; subtract 2h 21m for Dublin, 1h 26m for Greenock, 2h 29m for Liverpool.

D of M	D of W	Festivals, Events and Anniversaries	Sun at London Rises	Sun at London Sets	High Water at London am	High Water at London pm	Moon at London Rises	Moon at London Sets	Weather
			h m	h m	h m	h m	h m	h m	
1	F	*OED* published 1884	07:39	16:49	11 06	23 36	05 23	13 43	
2	Sa	Candlemas Day	07:37	16:51	—	12 01	06 15	14 33	
3	Su	Buddy Holly d. 1959	07:36	16:53	00 25	12 51	06 58	15 29	
4	M	World Cancer Day	07:34	16:54	01 10	13 35	07 34	16 29	
5	Tu	Chinese New Year (Pig)	07:32	16:56	01 50	14 15	08 05	17 32	
6	W	Access. Elizabeth II 1952	07:31	16:58	02 28	14 52	08 30	18 37	
7	Th	Hattie Jacques b. 1922	07:29	17:00	03 04	15 28	08 52	19 42	
8	F	Mary Queen of Scots executed 1587	07:27	17:02	03 38	16 02	09 12	20 48	
9	Sa	Princess Margaret d. 2002	07:26	17:04	04 12	16 37	09 31	21 54	
10	Su	YWCA founded 1870	07:24	17:05	04 47	17 14	09 50	23 02	
11	M	Whitney Houston d. 2012	07:22	17:07	05 24	17 54	10 11	—	
12	Tu	Vasco da Gama sails 1502	07:20	17:09	06 06	18 40	10 34	00 11	
13	W	Oliver Reed b. 1938	07:18	17:11	06 55	19 35	11 02	01 22	
14	Th	St Valentine	07:16	17:13	07 57	20 40	11 36	02 34	
15	F	Louis XV b. 1710	07:15	17:15	09 09	21 50	12 21	03 46	
16	Sa	Dick Bruna d. 2017	07:13	17:16	10 21	22 57	13 17	04 52	
17	Su	*Madama Butterfly* prem. 1904	07:11	17:18	11 28	23 57	14 26	05 51	
18	M	Clarence executed 1478	07:09	17:20	—	12 27	15 46	06 39	
19	Tu	Duke of York b. 1960	07:07	17:22	01 21	12 51	17 11	07 18	
20	W	Spacecraft *Mir* launched 1986	07:05	17:24	01 41	14 11	18 37	07 50	
21	Th	John Thaw d. 2002	07:03	17:25	02 29	14 59	20 01	08 17	
22	F	Kenneth Williams b 1926	07:01	17:27	03 15	15 45	21 23	08 41	
23	Sa	Stanley Matthews d. 2000	06:59	17:29	04 01	16 31	22 41	09 05	
24	Su	Castro retires 2008	06:57	17:31	04 47	17 17	23 57	09 29	
25	M	Bernard Bresslaw b. 1934	06:54	17:33	05 34	18 05	—	09 55	
26	Tu	Bonaparte escapes Elba 1815	06:52	17:34	06 24	18 56	01 09	10 25	
27	W	Labour party founded 1900	06:50	17:36	07 19	19 54	02 17	10 59	
28	Th	Joseph Bazalgette b. 1819	06:48	17:38	08 23	20 59	03 18	11 40	

Weather column (vertical text): A mild period will succeed the cold snap with at least 7–10 sunny days. Cold patches in the south. half will see individual cold days with erratic snow but often sunny again in the south.

MOON'S PHASES FEBRUARY 2019

		Days	Hours	Mins
●	New Moon	4	21	04
☽	First Quarter	12	22	26
○	Full Moon	19	15	53
☾	Last Quarter	26	11	28

All times on this page are GMT

PREDICTIONS

The New Moon on 4 February is in Aquarius in a conjunction with Mercury in the fifth house. This is a boom time for fashion and pop culture, with young British designers and writers poised for international fame. A high-tech communications start-up should be floated on the stock-exchange, with high profits to be made. The American government attempts to reboot itself with a raft of major reforms on democratic rights and immigration controls. The time is ripe for international peace treaties although talks will not be easy and will require give-and-take on all sides.

The Full Moon on 19 February falls in Virgo in a trine to Mars and Uranus on the tenth cusp. We can expect a major government reshuffle at the most senior level. In the economic sphere there should be a raft of new domestic financial regulations and reforms in the mortgage market. International trade agreements will turn out to be not what they seemed amid allegations of mismanagement. Fears of a trade war are high, but are unlikely to be realised. Nigeria is at high risk of revolution and a military take-over. Instability ripples across Africa and there may be talk of an 'African spring'.

At the *Betfair Ascot Chase*, a 5-year-old may be the winner. In Newbury, a 7-year-old carrying 11st 4lb may win the *Betfair Hurdle*, while a 6-year-old bearing 10st 4lb may win the Tote Gold Trophy.

UK Border Control

MARCH

For High Water add 5h 30m for Bristol, 4h 23m for Hull, 0h 43m for Leith; subtract 2h 21m for Dublin, 1h 26m for Greenock, 2h 29m for Liverpool.

D of M	D of W	Festivals, Events and Anniversaries	Sun at London Rises	Sun at London Sets	High Water at London Bridge am	High Water at London Bridge pm	Moon at London Rises	Moon at London Sets	Weather
			h m	h m	h m	h m	h m	h m	
1	F	St David's Day	06:46	17:40	09 33	22 06	04 12	12 28	Few surprises this month but northerly winds tend to dominate. This will result in a north-south weather divide, with parts of the south and south-west making a promising start to the spring.
2	Sa	Concorde's first flight 1969	06:44	17:41	10 41	23 08	04 58	13 22	
3	Su	Sir Henry Wood b. 1869	06:42	17:43	11 42	—	05 36	14 21	
4	M	Salisbury poisoning 2018	06:39	17:45	00 02	12 33	06 08	15 24	
5	Tu	Shrove Tuesday	06:37	17:47	00 49	13 16	06 34	16 28	
6	W	Ash Wednesday	06:35	17:48	01 30	13 55	06 57	17 34	
7	Th	Ranulph Fiennes b. 1934	06:33	17:50	02 06	14 30	07 18	18 40	
8	F	International Women's Day	06:31	17:52	02 40	15 03	07 37	19 46	
9	Sa	Yuri Gagarin b. 1934	06:28	17:54	03 13	15 36	07 56	20 54	
10	Su	Prince Edward b. 1964	06:26	17:55	03 46	16 09	08 16	22 02	
11	M	Commonwealth Day	06:24	17:57	04 20	16 44	08 38	23 12	
12	Tu	CofE female ordination 1994	06:21	17:59	04 57	17 23	09 03	—	
13	W	Phoenix Lights, Arizona 1997	06:20	18:01	05 38	18 06	09 34	00 23	
14	Th	Stephen Hawking d. 2018	06:17	18:02	06 27	18 59	10 13	01 33	
15	F	First domain name reg. 1985	06:15	18:04	07 28	20 05	11 03	02 40	
16	Sa	Theo Walcott b. 1989	06:13	18:06	08 43	21 20	12 04	03 39	
17	Su	St Patrick's Day	06:10	18:07	10 01	22 33	13 17	04 30	
18	M	Vesuvius erupts 1944	06:08	18:09	11 12	23 36	14 38	05 12	
19	Tu	Arthur C. Clarke d. 2008	06:06	18:11	—	12 13	16 02	05 46	
20	W	Spring equinox 21 58	06:04	18:13	00 33	13 06	17 27	06 14	
21	Th	Colin Dexter d. 2017	06:01	18:14	01 23	13 54	18 51	06 40	
22	F	A. Lloyd Webber b. 1948	05:59	18:16	02 10	14 39	20 14	07 04	
23	Sa	Pakistan a republic 1956	05:57	18:18	02 55	15 23	21 34	07 27	
24	Su	Mary Berry b. 1935	05:54	18:19	03 39	16 06	22 50	07 53	
25	M	Anunciation to Virgin Mary	05:52	18:21	04 23	16 49	—	08 22	
26	Tu	Aesop's Fables in print 1484	05:50	18:23	05 07	17 32	00 03	08 55	
27	W	Train robbers c'victed 1964	05:48	18:24	05 54	18 19	01 09	09 34	
28	Th	Sir Dirk Bogarde b. 1921	05:45	18:26	06 46	19 12	02 07	10 20	
29	F	UK leaves the EU	05:43	18:28	07 48	20 17	02 57	11 13	
30	Sa	Queen Mother d. 2002	05:41	18:29	09 01	21 28	03 38	12 11	
31	Su	Mothering Sunday	05:39	18:31	10 14	22 36	04 11	13 13	

MOON'S PHASES MARCH 2019			Days	Hours	Mins
	●	New Moon	6	16	04
	☽	First Quarter	14	10	27
	○	Full Moon	21	01	43
	☾	Last Quarter	28	04	10

All times on this page are GMT (Add 1 hr BST from 31st)

PREDICTIONS

The New Moon on 6 March is in Pisces in a conjunction with Neptune. This is a perfect indication for poets, prophets and dreamers, but very poor for all practical ventures in which detail will be ignored in favour of ideals. Continuing battles in the government may result in a shift of leadership to a younger generation. The Russian government benefits from increasing popularity which strengthens its hand in international negotiations.

The Full Moon on 21 March takes place in Libra in the ninth house at London. The square of Saturn and Pluto to the UK's Moon indicates the profound structural stress on financial and political institutions caused by Brexit, which is due on the 29th. Jupiter rising at London, however, indicates that the general national mood remains optimistic although there is no sign that splits between leavers and remainers will be resolved. There is still considerable doubt over the prospects of a soft Brexit at the end of an easy transition period. There is no sign of the promise that the people will take back control, and we will see continuing claims that government is trying to back-track on the referendum result. The risk of chaos at the borders remains high.

The *Cheltenham Gold Cup* may go to a 9-year-old favourite this month, whilst a 4-year-old carrying 10st 2lb may win the Imperial Cup at Sandown.

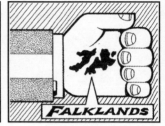

APRIL

For High Water add 5h 30m for Bristol, 4h 23m for Hull,
0h 43m for Leith; subtract 2h 21m for Dublin,
1h 26m for Greenock, 2h 29m for Liverpool.

D of M	D of W	Festivals, Events and Anniversaries	Sun at London Rises	Sun at London Sets	High Water at London Bridge am	High Water at London Bridge pm	Moon at London Rises	Moon at London Sets	Weather
			h m	h m	h m	h m	h m	h m	
1	M	April Fool's Day	05:36	18:33	11 16	23 33	04 39	14 17	
2	Tu	Penelope Keith b. 1939	05:34	18:34	—	12 08	05 03	15 23	
3	W	Pony Express op. 1860	05:32	18:36	00 21	12 50	05 24	16 29	
4	Th	NATO founded 1949	05:30	18:38	01 01	13 28	05 43	17 36	
5	F	Eric Bristow d. 2018	05:27	18:39	01 38	14 02	06 02	18 44	
6	Sa	Celuloid patent 1869	05:25	18:41	02 12	14 35	06 21	19 53	
7	Su	World Health Day	05:23	18:43	02 45	15 08	06 42	21 04	
8	M	Betty Ford b. 1918	05:21	18:44	03 19	15 42	07 06	22 16	
9	Tu	P. Charles m. Camilla 2005	05:18	18:46	03 55	16 18	07 35	23 07	
10	W	Sue Townsend d. 2014	05:16	18:48	04 33	16 58	08 11	—	
11	Th	William & Mary crowned 1689	05:14	18:49	05 17	17 42	08 57	00 34	
12	F	Union Flag adopted 1606	05:12	18:51	06 09	18 36	09 53	01 35	
13	Sa	Catherine de Medici b. 1519	05:10	18:53	07 12	19 42	11 00	02 28	
14	Su	Palm Sunday	05:07	18:54	08 28	20 58	12 16	03 11	
15	M	Kenneth Williams d. 1988	05:05	18:56	09 47	21 12	13 37	03 46	
16	Tu	Battle of Culloden 1746	05:03	18:58	10 56	23 16	14 59	04 15	
17	W	Ellis Island busiest day 1907	05:01	19:00	11 55	—	16 22	04 40	
18	Th	Dale Winton d. 2018	04:59	19:01	00 12	12 46	17 44	05 04	
19	F	Good Friday/Passover	04:57	19:03	01 02	13 33	19 05	05 27	
20	Sa	Curie's refine radium 1902	04:55	19:05	01 48	14 17	20 25	05 51	
21	Su	Easter Sun/Queen b. 1926	04:53	19:06	02 32	14 59	21 41	06 18	
22	M	Easter Monday	04:50	19:08	03 16	15 39	22 53	06 49	
23	Tu	St George/Pr. Louis b. 2018	04:48	19:10	03 58	16 20	23 57	07 26	
24	W	Duchess of Windsor d. 1986	04:46	19:11	04 41	17 01	—	08 10	
25	Th	Anzac Day	04:44	19:13	05 27	17 45	00 51	09 10	
26	F	Sid James d. 1976	04:42	19:14	06 17	18 35	01 36	09 59	
27	Sa	Passover ends	04:40	19:16	07 16	19 36	02 13	11 00	
28	Su	Low Sunday	04:38	19:18	08 26	20 47	02 43	12 04	
29	M	P William m. Catherine 2011	04:36	19:19	09 39	21 56	03 08	13 09	
30	Tu	Kirsten Dunst b. 1982	04:35	19:21	10 41	22 55	03 29	14 15	

Weather column (reading downward): Rainy windy days and cold nights give way to the month wet weather, thunderstorms and freak winds, especially central and south-east. At the turn of the month, maybe very warm, maybe a spell of warm, weather.

MOON'S PHASES APRIL 2019			Days	Hours	Mins
	●	New Moon	5	08	50
	☽	First Quarter	12	19	06
	○	Full Moon	19	11	12
	☾	Last Quarter	26	22	18

All times on this page are GMT (Add 1 hr BST)

PREDICTIONS

The New Moon on 5 April falls in Aries in the eleventh house at London and a wide square to Saturn and Pluto. The mood of the time favours romantics and dreamers. The government's 'confidence and supply' agreement with the DUP is in danger. Financial institutions are targeted by hidden enemies and the theft of major documents and revelation of scandals. The global focus shifts to Latin America. Cuba is in the middle of a democratic transition, and the leadership will pass to the younger generation. Argentina is in a period of prolonged instability and may renew its claim to the Malvinas/Falkland Islands, taking advantage of Brexit. The Venezulan government faces an international isolation refugee crisis.

The Full Moon on 19 April is in Libra in an opposition to Uranus pointing to general unpopularity for the government and possible defeat in by-elections and votes in the Commons. A property market swing will create uncertainty. Corruption scandals erupt in the Australian government and we may see ministerial resignations. The North Korean government is in a confused state suggesting that, with the right intention, peace deals may be struck.

The *Scottish Grand National* may go to a 9- or 10-year-old carrying 11st 9lb. At Aintree's *Grand National* look for a 9- or 10-year-old carrying 10st 7lb. The *Irish Grand National* could go to a 7-year-old carrying 10st 5lb.

MAY

For High Water add 5h 30m for Bristol, 4h 23m for Hull, 0h 43m for Leith; subtract 2h 21m for Dublin, 1h 26m for Greenock, 2h 29m for Liverpool.

D of M	D of W	Festivals, Events and Anniversaries	Sun at London Rises	Sun at London Sets	High Water at London Bridge am	High Water at London Bridge pm	Moon at London Rises	Moon at London Sets	Wea-ther
			h m	h m	h m	h m	h m	h m	
1	W	Arthur Wellesley b. 1769	04:33	19:23	11 32	23 44	03 49	15 22	
2	Th	Princess Charlotte b. 2015	04:31	19:24	—	12 16	04 07	16 30	
3	F	May uprising beg. 1849	04:29	19:26	00 26	12 54	04 26	17 39	
4	Sa	Star Wars day	04:27	19:28	01 04	13 29	04 46	18 51	
5	Su	First day of Ramadan	04:25	19:29	01 40	14 04	05 09	20 04	
6	M	Bank holiday	04:24	19:31	02 16	14 40	05 36	21 17	
7	Tu	Eva Peron b. 1919	04:22	19:32	02 54	15 16	06 10	22 27	
8	W	World Red Cross day	04:20	19:34	03 33	15 56	06 53	23 32	
9	Th	Joan Sims b. 1930	04:18	19:36	04 16	16 38	07 46	—	
10	F	Churchill PM 1940	04:17	19:37	05 04	17 26	08 50	00 28	
11	Sa	Cats op. London 1981	04:15	19:39	05 58	18 21	10 03	01 13	
12	Su	Perry Como d. 2001	04:13	19:40	07 03	19 26	11 22	01 50	
13	M	Daphne du Maurier b. 1907	04:12	19:42	08 16	20 39	12 42	02 19	
14	Tu	Eric Morecambe b. 1926	04:10	19:43	09 30	21 50	14 02	02 45	
15	W	L. Frank Baum b. 1856	04:09	19:45	10 36	22 53	15 22	03 08	
16	Th	First Oscars 1929	04:07	19:46	11 33	23 48	16 42	03 30	
17	F	Last Liberal gov. ends 1915	04:06	19:48	—	12 23	18 01	03 52	
18	Sa	UN moves to NYC 1951	04:04	19:49	00 38	13 09	19 19	04 17	
19	Su	Vesak Day	04:03	19:51	01 25	13 52	20 33	04 45	
20	M	Armada sailed 1588	04:02	19:52	02 09	14 33	21 41	05 19	
21	Tu	Bogart m. Bacall 1945	04:00	19:54	02 52	15 14	22 41	06 00	
22	W	Manchester attack 2017	03:59	19:55	03 35	15 53	23 32	06 49	
23	Th	Roger Moore d. 2017	03:58	19:56	04 17	16 34	—	07 44	
24	F	Queen Victoria b. 1819	03:57	19:58	05 02	17 17	00 12	08 45	
25	Sa	HMS Pinafore op. 1878	03:56	19:59	05 50	18 03	00 45	09 49	
26	Su	Rogation Sunday	03:55	20:00	06 44	18 58	01 12	10 54	
27	M	Spring Bank Holiday	03:54	20:02	07 47	20 01	01 35	12 00	
28	Tu	First IoM TT Race 1907	03:53	20:03	08 53	21 07	01 54	13 06	
29	W	Charles II b. 1630	03:52	20:04	09 55	22 07	02 13	14 13	
30	Th	Ascension Day	03:51	20:05	10 48	22 58	02 31	15 22	
31	F	Battle of Jutland 1916	03:50	20:06	11 34	23 44	02 50	16 32	

Weather column (vertical): Warm day temperatures early and late in the month (except northern Scotland), before heavy rains nearly everywhere toward the close. Traditional May night frosts should not be ruled out.

MOON'S PHASES MAY 2019		Days	Hours	Mins
●	New Moon	4	22	45
☽	First Quarter	12	01	12
○	Full Moon	18	21	11
☾	Last Quarter	26	16	33

All times on this page are GMT (Add 1 hr BST)

PREDICTIONS

The New Moon on 4 May is in Taurus in the fifth house, in a trine to Saturn and Pluto. Jupiter and Mars are on the horizon at London indicating that the time is right for crusades. There will be a spate of moral panics, and principle takes priority over practical politics. The Balkans are in a period of change, thanks to Russian interference. Bosnia is experiencing renewed communal tensions as Serbian nationalists attempt to seize control of parts of the country. Serbia will take a step closer to joining the EU. Tensions also rise across south-east Asia. We can expect international pressure on Myanmar and a change at the top of the government. Vietnam is experiencing an economic boom and should be a prime target for investors.

The Full Moon on 18 May is in Scorpio in the twelfth house at London. Financial indicators are generally positive, although the fact that the markets may reach a peak also points to a short fall in coming weeks. Health spending will rise, with more funds for mental health. New regulations will be introduced in areas of gender and transgender rights. The Philippines is engaged in talks with China over new security co-operation, establishing a new balance of power.

The winner at Newmarket's *2,000 Guineas* (for 3-year-olds) could be ridden by an American jockey, while the *1,000 Guineas* should see a firm favourite as victor.

JUNE

For High Water add 5h 30m for Bristol, 4h 23m for Hull, 0h 43m for Leith; subtract 2h 21m for Dublin, 1h 26m for Greenock, 2h 29m for Liverpool.

D of M	D of W	Festivals, Events and Anniversaries	Sun at London Rises	Sun at London Sets	High Water at London Bridge am	High Water at London Bridge pm	Moon at London Rises	Moon at London Sets	Weather
			h m	h m	h m	h m	h m	h m	
1	Sa	Int'ional Children's Day	03:49	20:07	—	12 15	03 12	17 45	
2	Su	Peter Sallis d. 2017	03:48	20:08	00 27	12 55	03 37	18 59	
3	M	Tony Curtis b. 1925	03:47	20:10	01 08	13 34	04 08	20 13	
4	Tu	End of Ramadan (Eid al-Fitr)	03:47	20:11	01 49	14 14	04 47	21 22	
5	W	Noddy in print 1949	03:46	20:11	02 32	14 55	05 37	22 23	
6	Th	Kenneth Connor b. 1918	03:45	20:12	03 16	15 38	06 39	23 13	
7	F	Lusitania launched 1906	03:45	20:13	04 03	16 24	07 51	23 53	
8	Sa	Shavuot begins	03:44	20:14	04 54	17 14	09 09	—	
9	Su	Pentecost	03:44	20:15	05 50	18 09	10 30	00 25	
10	M	Duke of Edinburgh b. 1921	03:44	20:16	06 52	19 12	11 50	00 51	
11	Tu	Bernard Bresslaw d. 1993	03:43	20:16	08 00	20 19	1 309	01 14	
12	W	A Frank begins diary 1942	03:43	20:17	09 08	21 25	14 27	01 36	
13	Th	Peasants' Revolt 1381	03:43	20:18	10 11	22 28	15 45	01 57	
14	F	Grenfell Tower fire 2017	03:42	20:18	11 08	23 24	17 01	02 20	
15	Sa	Magna Carta sealed 1215	03:42	20:19	11 59	—	18 16	02 46	
16	Su	Father's Day	03:42	20:19	00 15	12 45	19 26	03 17	
17	M	Edward I b. 1239	03:42	20:20	01 03	13 29	20 30	03 54	
18	Tu	Earhart flew Atlantic 1928	03:42	20:20	01 49	14 10	21 24	04 39	
19	W	Nicene Creed presented 325AD	03:42	20:20	02 32	14 51	22 09	05 32	
20	Th	Corpus Christi	03:42	20:21	03 14	15 30	22 46	06 31	
21	F	Solstice (16 54)/Pr. Will born	03:43	20:21	03 57	16 10	23 15	07 34	
22	Sa	George V c'nation 1911	03:43	20:21	04 39	16 51	23 39	08 39	
23	Su	UK votes to leave EU 2016	03:43	20:21	05 23	17 34	—	09 45	
24	M	Feast of John the Baptist	03:43	20:21	06 10	18 21	00 00	10 51	
25	Tu	Johnny Herbert b. 1964	03:44	20:21	07 02	19 13	00 18	11 57	
26	W	Presley final concert 1977	03:44	20:21	08 00	20 11	00 36	13 04	
27	Th	Michael Bond d. 2017	03:45	20:21	08 59	21 11	00 55	14 12	
28	F	Treaty of Versailles 1919	03:45	20:21	09 56	22 09	01 14	15 23	
29	Sa	UK Armed Forces Day	03:46	20:21	10 48	23 02	01 37	16 36	
30	Su	Tower Bridge op. 1894	03:46	20:21	11 36	23 52	02 05	17 51	

Summer at its finest and warmest for most of Britain early to mid-month and at the close. Third week may see thundery rainfall causing local flooding in parts of the south and Midlands.

MOON'S PHASES JUNE 2019

		Days	Hours	Mins
●	New Moon	3	10	02
☽	First Quarter	10	05	59
○	Full Moon	17	08	31
☾	Last Quarter	25	09	46

All times on this page are GMT (Add 1 hr BST)

PREDICTIONS

The New Moon on 3 June falls in Gemini in a tense 'T' square with Neptune and Jupiter, indicating good prospects for growth. The public mood is positive. Potentially profitable investments include high-tech transportation systems. More funds will be promised to the school system, including using education for crime prevention. Hopes rise for new gene cures for long-standing medical problems. The European Union takes significant steps towards major economic and banking integration, and records higher growth figures. Pressure on the South African government mounts as hopes of reform are disappointed, but new proposals for land reform are widely greeted.

The Full Moon on 17 June is in Sagittarius in an optimistic conjunction with Jupiter, pointing to general confidence. However, Mars and Mercury are in a tough opposition to Saturn and Pluto indicating risk of a health crisis, and the threat of new, untreatable diseases. The risk of war is at a peak and it is vital that the greatest effort possible be put into diplomacy and the avoidance of potential accidents. India steps up to become a global economic power with investment and growth at record rates. Western Australia is at renewed risk of environmental chaos and flooding.

Look out for an Irish trained horse at the *Derby* this year, especially ridden by a southern jockey. At this year's *Oaks* in Epsom (for 3-year-old fillies) an outsider may achieve a surprise win.

JULY

For High Water add 5h 30m for Bristol, 4h 23m for Hull, 0h 43m for Leith; subtract 2h 21m for Dublin, 1h 26m for Greenock, 2h 29m for Liverpool.

D of M	D of W	Festivals, Events and Anniversaries	Sun at London Rises	Sun at London Sets	High Water at London Bridge am	High Water at London Bridge pm	Moon at London Rises	Moon at London Sets	Weather
			h m	h m	h m	h m	h m	h m	A cool, sometimes rainy, start will be followed by further heat, with very high temperatures mid-month, giving rise to fierce localised thunderstorms. Cooler and wet at the close, with north-west wind.
1	M	Princess Diana b. 1961	03:47	20:20	—	12 22	02 40	19 03	
2	Tu	Total solar eclipse (19 22)	03:48	20:20	00 40	13 07	03 25	20 09	
3	W	Tom Cruise b. 1962	03:48	20:20	01 27	13 51	04 23	21 06	
4	Th	US Independence Day	03:49	20:19	02 15	14 36	05 33	21 51	
5	F	Dolly the Sheep b. 1996	03:50	20:19	03 03	15 23	06 52	22 27	
6	Sa	Richard III coronation 1483	03:51	20:18	03 52	16 10	08 14	22 56	
7	Su	7/7 terrorist attacks 2005	03:52	20:18	04 43	17 01	09 36	23 20	
8	M	Betty Ford d. 2011	03:53	20:17	05 37	17 54	10 57	23 43	
9	Tu	Barbara Cartland b. 1901	03:54	20:16	06 34	18 52	12 16	—	
10	W	John Calvin b. 1509	03:55	20:16	07 36	19 54	13 34	00 04	
11	Th	Lord Olivier d. 1989	03:56	20:15	08 39	20 58	14 50	00 26	
12	F	Orangemen's Day (hol) NI	03:57	20:14	09 42	22 01	16 04	00 51	
13	Sa	Ian Hislop b. 1960	03:58	20:13	10 40	23 00	17 15	01 19	
14	Su	Bastille Day (France)	03:59	20:12	11 34	23 55	18 20	01 53	
15	M	St Swithin's Day	04:00	20:11	—	12 23	19 18	02 34	
16	Tu	Partial lunar eclipse (21 30)	04:01	20:10	00 45	13 08	20 06	03 24	
17	W	Duchess of Cornwall b. 1947	04:02	20:09	01 31	13 50	20 45	04 20	
18	Th	Ballot Act 1872	04:04	20:08	02 15	14 31	21 17	05 22	
19	F	*Mary Rose* sinks 1545	04:05	20:07	02 56	15 10	21 43	06 27	
20	Sa	*Apollo* 11 lunar landing 1969	04:06	20:06	03 36	15 48	22 04	07 33	
21	Su	Battle of Shrewsbury 1403	04:08	20:04	04 15	16 26	22 24	08 38	
22	M	Prince George b. 2013	04:09	20:03	04 54	17 04	22 42	09 44	
23	Tu	Pr Andrew m. Sarah 1986	04:10	20:02	05 34	17 44	22 59	10 50	
24	W	Speaking clock begins 1936	04:12	20:01	06 17	18 27	23 18	11 56	
25	Th	Mary I m. Philip II 1554	04:13	19:59	07 06	19 18	23 39	13 05	
26	F	George B Shaw b. 1856	04:14	19:58	08 01	20 16	—	14 15	
27	Sa	Geneva Convention 1929	04:16	19:56	09 02	21 20	00 03	15 28	
28	Su	Post codes introduced 1959	04:17	19:55	10 02	22 24	00 34	16 40	
29	M	Charles and Diana m. 1981	04:19	19:53	11 00	23 23	01 13	17 49	
30	Tu	Otto von Bismarck d. 1898	04:20	19:52	11 53	—	02 04	18 51	
31	W	J. K. Rowling b. 1965	04:22	19:50	00 18	12 44	03 09	19 42	

MOON'S PHASES JULY 2019		Days	Hours	Mins
● New Moon		2	19	16
☽ First Quarter		9	10	55
○ Full Moon		16	21	38
☾ Last Quarter		25	01	18

All times on this page are GMT (Add 1 hr BST)

PREDICTIONS

The New Moon on 2 July is in Cancer in the seventh house, opposed to Saturn and Pluto. Nationalist sentiments are at a height leading to moves across the world to restrict immigration and deport aliens. The eclipse path is total over Buenos Aires inaugurating a chance of major reform in Argentina, which could become an economic powerhouse of the southern hemisphere. Jupiter is on the Midheaven of the chart for German economic reunification pointing to very strong growth, and the Eurozone is experiencing a period of stability. Greece is beginning to emerge from its financial troubles, and job creation proceeds apace.

The Full Moon on 16 July is an eclipse in Capricorn, conjunct Saturn and Pluto in the twelfth house. There is a risk of sabotage in the mining and power industries and a risk of new epidemics. Iran may be the object of military attacks by its neighbours and threats to its integrity, although there is no threat to the government from within the country. There are fresh international attempts to nation-build in Somalia and the Horn of Africa, driving out the jihadis.

A 6-year-old is the likely winner in the *Goodwood Cup* whilst a 4-year-old bearing 9st 1lb may win in the *Stewards' Cup* handicap. The *International Stakes* at Ascot may go to a 4-year-old carrying 10st 1lb. The *Darley July Cup* may be won by a 4-year-old carrying 9st 7lb.

AUGUST

For High Water add 5h 30m for Bristol, 4h 23m for Hull, 0h 43m for Leith; subtract 2h 21m for Dublin, 1h 26m for Greenock, 2h 29m for Liverpool.

D of M	D of W	Festivals, Events and Anniversaries	Sun at London Rises	Sun at London Sets	High Water at London Bridge am	High Water at London Bridge pm	Moon at London Rises	Moon at London Sets	Weather
			h m	h m	h m	h m	h m	h m	
1	Th	Act of Union 1800	04:23	19:49	01 10	13 32	04 25	20 23	Fewer regional variations in weather, but generally better conditions in the south and east than elsewhere. No outstandingly hot or fine spell. Frequent day-to-day changes during each week.
2	F	Shimon Peres b. 1923	04:25	19:47	02 00	14 20	05 49	20 56	
3	Sa	Robert Hardy d. 2017	04:26	19:45	02 49	15 07	07 14	21 23	
4	Su	Meghan Markle b. 1981	04:28	19:44	03 37	15 54	08 39	21 47	
5	M	Bank holiday (Scotland)	04:29	19:42	04 26	16 43	10 01	22 09	
6	Tu	Barbara Windsor b. 1937	04:31	19:40	05 17	17 33	11 21	22 31	
7	W	Last US lynching 1930	04:32	19:38	06 09	18 27	12 39	22 55	
8	Th	Princess Beatrice b. 1988	04:34	19:36	07 05	19 25	13 55	23 22	
9	F	Sistine Chapel op. 1483	04:35	19:35	08 06	20 29	15 07	23 54	
10	Sa	Magellan set sail 1519	04:37	19:33	09 09	21 35	16 14	—	
11	Su	Enid Blyton b. 1897	04:39	19:31	10 12	22 39	17 13	00 33	
12	M	Grouse shooting season op.	04:40	19:29	11 11	23 38	18 04	01 19	
13	Tu	Madhur Jaffrey b. 1933	04:42	19:27	—	12 03	18 45	02 13	
14	W	VJ Day 1945	04:43	19:25	00 30	12 49	19 19	03 13	
15	Th	Princess Royal b. 1950	04:45	19:23	01 16	13 32	19 47	04 17	
16	F	Elvis Presley d. 1977	04:47	19:21	01 58	14 11	20 09	05 23	
17	Sa	*Animal Farm* pub. 1945	04:48	19:19	02 36	14 48	20 29	06 28	
18	Su	Bruce Forsyth d. 2017	04:50	19:17	03 13	15 24	20 47	07 34	
19	M	World Humanitarian Day	04:51	19:15	03 48	15 58	21 05	08 40	
20	Tu	Prince Albert b. 1819	04:53	19:13	04 22	16 33	21 23	09 45	
21	W	Princess Margaret b. 1930	04:54	19:11	04 58	17 08	21 42	10 52	
22	Th	Battle of Bosworth 1485	04:56	19:09	05 36	17 48	22 04	12 01	
23	F	Albert Bdge, London op. 1873	04:58	19:07	06 19	18 34	22 31	13 11	
24	Sa	Feast of St Bartholomew	05:59	19:05	07 10	19 31	23 05	14 22	
25	Su	Paris liberated 1944	05:01	19:02	08 12	20 40	23 49	15 31	
26	M	Summer bank holiday	05:02	19:00	09 21	21 53	—	16 34	
27	Tu	Don Bradman b. 1908	05:04	18:58	10 28	23 01	00 46	17 30	
28	W	2nd Battle Bull Run 1862	05:06	18:56	11 29	—	01 56	18 15	
29	Th	Michael Jackson b. 1958	05:07	18:54	00 01	12 24	03 16	18 51	
30	F	Evacuation begins 1939	05:09	18:52	00 55	13 14	04 42	19 21	
31	Sa	Princess Diana d. 1997	05:10	18:49	01 45	14 02	06 09	19 47	

			Days	Hours	Mins
MOON'S	●	New Moon	1	03	12
PHASES	☽	First Quarter	7	17	31
AUGUST	○	Full Moon	15	12	29
2019	☾	Last Quarter	23	14	56
	●	New Moon	30	10	37

All times on this page are GMT (Add 1 hr BST)

PREDICTIONS

The New Moon on 1 August is in Leo, in a conjunction with Mars and Venus, pointing to passion, creativity and commercial success in the artistic sectors. This is a peak moment for innovation across the board and it's an auspicious moment to form unusual partnerships, social enterprises and companies which aim to disrupt established production cycles. The emphasis is on the sustainable 'circular economy' in which recycling is mandatory.

The Full Moon on 15 August takes place in Aquarius in an opposition to Venus and Mars. Struggles within the government produce a challenge to the Prime Minister. The French government is passing through a period of instability, but should be able to force through union and labour reforms. Colombia is the country to note in Latin America, and may assume a leading role in resolving regional problems and offering a prime opportunity for investors.

The New Moon on 30 August falls in Virgo, in a powerful conjunction with Mars and Venus. There will be a wholesale reorganisation in the government with new ministries created and others merged, but confusing results may lead to a decline in public trust. India is at risk from communal tensions and steps need to be taken to avert Hindu–Muslim clashes.

In York's *Ebor Handicap* a 4-year-old carrying 8st 6lb–9st may win. A 5-year-old carrying 9st 8lb may win Goodwood's *King George Stakes*.

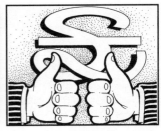

SEPTEMBER

For High Water add 5h 30m for Bristol, 4h 23m for Hull, 0h 43m for Leith; subtract 2h 21m for Dublin, 1h 26m for Greenock, 2h 29m for Liverpool.

D of M	D of W	Festivals, Events and Anniversaries	Sun at London Rises	Sun at London Sets	High Water at London Bridge am	High Water at London Bridge pm	Moon at London Rises	Moon at London Sets	Weather
			h m	h m	h m	h m	h m	h m	
1	Su	Islamic New Year	05:12	18:47	02 32	14 49	07 35	20 10	
2	M	Great Fire of London 1666	05:14	18:45	03 19	15 35	09 00	20 33	
3	Tu	Merchant Navy Day	05:15	18:43	04 05	16 21	10 22	20 57	
4	W	Joan Rivers d. 2014	05:17	18:40	04 51	17 09	11 41	21 23	
5	Th	Great Fire 1666 ends	05:18	18:38	05 04	17 59	12 56	21 54	
6	F	Hurricane Irma 2017	05:20	18:36	06 31	18 55	14 06	22 31	
7	Sa	Khrushchev elected 1953	05:22	18:34	07 29	19 59	15 09	23 16	
8	Su	George III m. Charlotte 1761	05:23	18:31	08 34	21 10	16 03	—	
9	M	Leo Tolstoy b. 1828	05:25	18:29	09 43	22 20	16 47	00 07	
10	Tu	William Bligh b. 1754	05:26	18:27	10 47	23 22	17 22	01 06	
11	W	9/11 2001	05:28	18:25	11 42	—	17 51	02 09	
12	Th	Jesse Owens b. 1913	05:29	18:22	00 14	12 30	18 15	03 14	
13	F	Buckingham P. bombed 1940	05:31	18:20	00 58	13 12	18 35	04 19	
14	Sa	Arthur Wellesley d. 1852	05:33	18:18	01 37	13 49	0:00	05 25	
15	Su	Prince Harry b. 1984	05:34	18:15	02 13	14 24	19 11	06 31	
16	M	*Mayflower* sails 1620	05:36	18:13	02 47	14 57	19 29	07 37	
17	Tu	Paula Yates d. 2000	05:37	18:11	03 19	15 29	19 47	08 44	
18	W	Tiffany & Co. op. 1837	05:39	18:08	03 51	16 02	20 08	09 52	
19	Th	Hurricane Maria 2017	05:41	18:06	04 25	16 37	20 32	11 01	
20	F	Marc Bolan d. 1977	05:42	18:04	05 01	17 16	21 03	12 10	
21	Sa	International Day of Peace	05:44	18:01	05 42	18 01	21 42	13 19	
22	Su	Michael Faraday b. 1791	05:45	17:59	06 31	18 59	22 31	14 23	
23	M	Autumn equinox (08 50)	05:47	17:57	07 33	20 12	23 34	15 20	
24	Tu	Theo Paphitis b. 1959	05:49	17:55	08 48	21 32	—	16 08	
25	W	Liz Dawn d. 2017	05:50	17:52	10 02	22 44	00 47	16 47	
26	Th	Serena Williams b. 1981	05:52	17:50	11 08	23 45	02 09	17 19	
27	F	Wm Conqueror sails 1066	05:54	17:48	—	12 04	03 45	17 45	
28	Sa	Brigitte Bardot b. 1934	05:55	17:45	00 39	12 55	05 02	18 09	
29	Su	Michaelmas/Rosh Hashanah	05:57	17:43	01 27	13 43	06 28	18 32	
30	M	*Magic Flute* debuts 1791	05:58	17:41	02 12	14 28	07 54	18 56	

Weather column (spanning): will be everywhere. North-west winds will be strong in an unsettled pattern. North-west winds will be followed by an unsettled pattern. Summer extends for 10–12 days, bringing gales during the final week and cool temperatures everywhere.

MOON'S PHASES SEPTEMBER 2019			Days	Hours	Mins
	☽	First Quarter	6	03	10
	○	Full Moon	14	04	33
	☾	Last Quarter	22	02	41
	●	New Moon	28	18	26

All times on this page are GMT (Add 1 hr BST)

PREDICTIONS

The Full Moon on 14 September is in Pisces conjunct Neptune and opposed Mars. This is a positive period for free spirits, mystics and spiritual thinkers, but very poor for initiatives which require clarity, efficiency and clear targets. In Europe tensions focus on the Baltics and the former communist states of the East, with fears of Russian interference in Estonia, Latvia and Lithuania. We may expect a change of government in Poland. Latin America may also be in turmoil and regime change is possible in Bolivia and Venezuela. There are new fears that Colombia and Peru are again in danger of becoming narco-states, controlled by international drug cartels. In Cuba a new, popular, young leadership finally takes over.

The New Moon on 28 September is in Libra in a constructive aspect with revolutionary Uranus on the ascendant. Saturn is on the Midheaven at London, indicating difficulties in the government and probably u-turns on major policy initiatives. Internationally, Mexico is in the news with major protests against the killing of journalists and opposition politicians. Underlying trends in the global economy continue to be buoyant in spite of short-term fluctuations. Good stocks are centred on communication and travel including space exploration.

In the *St. Leger* meeting at Doncaster the victor may be a favourite trained in the Midlands, whilst a 5-year-old carrying 10st 4lb may win the *Gold Cup* at Ayr.

OCTOBER

For High Water add 5h 30m for Bristol, 4h 23m for Hull, 0h 43m for Leith; subtract 2h 21m for Dublin, 1h 26m for Greenock, 2h 29m for Liverpool.

D of M	D of W	Festivals, Events and Anniversaries	Sun at London Rises	Sun at London Sets	High Water at London Bridge am	High Water at London Bridge pm	Moon at London Rises	Moon at London Sets	Wea- ther
			h m	h m	h m	h m	h m	h m	
1	Tu	Theresa May b. 1956	06:00	17:39	02 57	15 13	09 17	19 21	
2	W	Mahatma Gandhi b. 1869	06:02	17:36	03 40	15 58	10 37	19 51	
3	Th	OJ Simpson acquitted 1995	06:03	17:34	04 24	16 43	11 53	20 26	
4	F	Rembrandt d. 1669	06:05	17:32	05 09	17 32	13 01	21 09	
5	Sa	*Dr. No* released 1962	06:07	17:29	05 57	18 25	13 59	21 59	
6	Su	Hattie Jacques d. 1980	06:08	17:27	06 51	19 28	14 57	22 57	
7	M	Carbon paper patent 1806	06:10	17:25	07 56	20 42	15 25	23 59	
8	Tu	Yom Kippur	06:12	17:23	09 09	21 56	15 56	—	
9	W	Donald Sinden b. 1923	06:13	17:21	10 18	23 00	16 21	01 04	
10	Th	Great Hurricane 1780	06:15	17:18	11 16	23 51	16 42	02 09	
11	F	Henry Heinz b. 1844	06:17	17:16	—	12 04	17 01	03 16	
12	Sa	Crown Jewels lost 1216	06:18	17:14	00 34	12 45	17 18	04 22	
13	Su	Lillie Langtry b. 1853	06:20	17:12	01 11	13 22	17 35	05 28	
14	M	Battle of Hastings 1066	06:22	17:10	01 45	13 56	17 53	06 35	
15	Tu	PG Wodehouse b. 1881	06:23	17:07	02 18	14 28	18 13	07 43	
16	W	*Jane Eyre* pub. 1847	06:25	17:05	02 49	15 01	18 36	08 53	
17	Th	Al Capone convicted 1931	06:27	17:03	03 22	15 34	19 04	10 03	
18	F	Feast of St Luke	06:28	17:01	03 56	16 11	19 39	11 12	
19	Sa	King John d. 1216	06:30	16:59	04 33	16 52	20 24	12 18	
20	Su	Last Day of Sukkot	06:32	16:57	05 15	17 40	21 21	13 16	
21	M	Aberfan disaster 1966	06:34	16:55	06 05	18 39	22 29	14 06	
22	Tu	Joan Fontaine b. 1917	06:35	16:53	07 07	19 54	23 45	14 56	
23	W	Battle of Edgehill 1642	06:37	16:51	08 23	21 15	—	15 19	
24	Th	United Nations Day	06:39	16:49	09 39	22 27	01 07	15 46	
25	F	Geoffrey Chaucer d. 1400	06:41	16:47	10 46	23 27	02 31	16 10	
26	Sa	Pony Express closes 1821	06:42	16:45	11 43	—	03 56	16 32	
27	Su	Diwali	06:44	16:43	00 19	12 34	05 21	16 55	
28	M	Auguste Escoffier b. 1846	06:46	16:41	01 07	13 22	06 46	17 19	
29	Tu	Raleigh beheaded 1618	06:48	16:39	01 51	14 07	08 09	17 46	
30	W	Henry VII crowned 1485	06:49	16:37	02 34	14 51	09 30	18 19	
31	Th	Hallowe'en	06:51	16:35	03 16	15 35	10 44	18 59	

The often-looked-for mid-month return to a handful of summerlike days may occur this year and not disappoint. Going into the final week conditions may turn unsettled, with storms likely.

MOON'S PHASES OCTOBER 2019			Days	Hours	Mins
☽	First Quarter		5	16	47
○	Full Moon		13	21	08
☾	Last Quarter		21	12	39
●	New Moon		28	03	38

All times on this page are GMT (BST to 27 October + 1 hour)

PREDICTIONS

The Full Moon on 13 October falls in Aries in a difficult 'T' square with the Sun, Saturn and Pluto. Globally, confrontation is the norm, with increasing tension over the coming weeks. The UK government is involved in a spate of foreign policy problems, finding its ambitions blocked at every turn. There are fears that the UK will lose key overseas markets, with potential job losses in most sectors. New border controls will cause problems for marketers. Change is due in the countries of East Africa. Tanzania and Kenya are both returning positive growth figures, but an increasingly prosperous population requires greater freedoms, and consequently we may see protests.

The New Moon on 28 October is in Scorpio in the second house, in an opposition to Uranus in the eighth. Financial institutions will be under maximum stress and regulators should prepare for banking failures. Political earthquakes may be seen across Left and Right. Headlines will announce that nobody could have predicted this month's events. Political upsets may be seen in the Midwest of the USA, Central America and south-east Asia, where elections will be won by outsiders, and incumbents should lose.

Look for a 4-year-old carrying 10st at the *Cesarewitch Heritage Handicap* and a well-fancied 3-year-old at the *Cambridgeshire*. A 3-year-old carrying 9st 5lb may win at Ascot's *Queen Elizabeth II Stakes*.

Leadership Contest

SPACE MILITERISATION

NOVEMBER

For High Water add 5h 30m for Bristol, 4h 23m for Hull, 0h 43m for Leith; subtract 2h 21m for Dublin, 1h 26m for Greenock, 2h 29m for Liverpool.

D of M	D of W	Festivals, Events and Anniversaries	Sun at London Rises	Sun at London Sets	High Water at London Bridge am	High Water at London Bridge pm	Moon at London Rises	Moon at London Sets	Wea- ther
			h m	h m	h m	h m	h m	h m	
1	F	All Saints' Day	06:53	16:34	03 58	16 20	11 49	19 47	Expect mostly windy and frequently rainy weather early and late but some warm and sunny episodes in between. Mostly dry except in the north, with some unusually mild days in the south.
2	Sa	Day of the Dead, Mexico	06:55	16:32	04 40	17 06	12 43	20 43	
3	Su	Arno floods 1966	06:56	16:30	05 25	17 57	13 26	21 45	
4	M	Tutankhamun disc. 1922	06:58	16:28	06 16	18 57	13 59	22 50	
5	Tu	Bonfire Night	07:00	16:27	07 17	20 09	14 26	23 57	
6	W	Emma Stone b. 1988	07:02	16:25	08 29	21 22	14 48	—	
7	Th	Eleanor Roosevelt d. 1962	07:03	16:23	09 39	22 25	15 07	01 03	
8	F	Ken Dodd b. 1931	07:05	16:22	10 39	23 18	15 25	02 09	
9	Sa	Edward VII b. 1841	07:07	16:20	11 29	—	15 42	03 16	
10	Su	Remembrance Sunday	07:09	16:18	00 01	12 12	15 59	04 23	
11	M	Mercury transit (15 19)	07:10	16:17	00 39	12 50	16 18	05 31	
12	Tu	Ellis Island closed 1954	07:12	16:15	01 14	13 25	16 39	06 41	
13	W	*Fantasia* released 1940	07:14	16:14	01 48	13 59	17 06	07 52	
14	Th	Prince of Wales b. 1948	07:16	16:13	02 22	14 35	17 39	09 04	
15	F	Mugabe arrested 2017	07:17	16:11	02 56	15 12	18 21	10 12	
16	Sa	Edward Woodward d. 2009	07:19	16:10	03 33	15 53	19 14	11 14	
17	Su	Mary I d. 1558	07:21	16:08	04 13	16 37	20 19	12 06	
18	M	Ant McPartlin b. 1975	07:22	16:07	04 57	17 28	21 32	12 49	
19	Tu	UK lottery begins 1994	07:24	16:06	05 48	18 28	22 50	13 23	
20	W	Pr. Elizabeth m. Philip 1947	07:26	16:05	06 50	19 39	—	13 51	
21	Th	David Cassidy d. 2017	07:27	16:04	08 01	20 55	00 11	14 15	
22	F	George Eliot b. 1819	07:29	16:03	09 15	22 04	01 33	14 36	
23	Sa	John Major PM 1990	07:31	16:01	10 22	23 04	02 55	14 57	
24	Su	*Origin of Species* pub. 1859	07:32	16:00	11 20	23 57	04 18	15 19	
25	M	Joe DiMaggio b. 1914	07:34	15:59	—	12 12	05 40	15 44	
26	Tu	Cyril Cusack b. 1910	07:35	15:59	00 45	13 01	07 02	16 13	
27	W	Buster Merryfield b. 1920	07:37	15:58	01 29	13 47	08 20	16 49	
28	Th	Thanksgiving (USA)	07:38	15:57	02 12	14 31	09 31	17 34	
29	F	Cardinal Wolsey d. 1530	07:40	15:56	02 53	15 15	10 32	18 27	
30	Sa	St Andrew's Day	07:41	15:55	03 34	15 59	11 21	19 28	

MOON'S PHASES NOVEMBER 2019		Days	Hours	Mins
☽	First Quarter	4	10	23
○	Full Moon	12	13	34
☾	Last Quarter	19	21	11
●	New Moon	26	15	06

All times on this page are GMT

PREDICTIONS

The Full Moon on 12 November falls in Taurus in a stressful opposition to Mercury and a harmonious trine to Saturn and Pluto. In London, Parliament is in turmoil and the government will lose significant votes and elections. Globally, the time is right for tough-talking to solve deep problems, and we may see high profile rounds of shuttle diplomacy between Washington, Moscow and Beijing. The Middle East peace process will be revived with support from Egypt and Saudi Arabia. Iranian influence will be at a low-point anywhere except over its own clients, Hamas and Hezbollah. In Israel the opposition is fragmented and the government free to take whatever actions it pleases. The South African government faces turmoil as covered-up scandals are revealed.

The New Moon on 26 November is in Sagittarius in the seventh house in a semi-sextile to Mars and a quincunx to Uranus. Renewed turmoil hits the UK government, and there is a high probability of a leadership contest and the threat of an early general election. On the international scene, space travel takes a major leap forward, although there are fears of the militarisation of space. We may also expect a major space achievement by Russian cosmonauts, perhaps preparations for a Mars mission.

A well-fancied 3-year-old carrying 8st 8lbs could win the Doncaster *November Handicap*. A 4-year-old bearing 9st 1lb may win the Newbury *Gold Cup Chase*.

DECEMBER

For High Water add 5h 30m for Bristol, 4h 23m for Hull, 0h 43m for Leith; subtract 2h 21m for Dublin, 1h 26m for Greenock, 2h 29m for Liverpool.

D of M	D of W	Festivals, Events and Anniversaries	Sun at London Rises	Sun at London Sets	High Water at London Bridge am	High Water at London Bridge pm	Moon at London Rises	Moon at London Sets	Weather
			h m	h m	h m	h m	h m	h m	
1	Su	Advent	07:43	15:55	04 16	16 44	11 59	20 33	
2	M	Britney Spears b. 1981	07:44	15:54	04 59	17 32	12 29	21 40	
3	Tu	Eamonn Holmes b. 1953	07:46	15:54	05 46	18 25	12 53	22 48	
4	W	Christine Keeler d. 2017	07:47	15:53	06 39	19 26	13 13	23 54	
5	Th	Walt Disney b. 1901	07:48	15:53	07 41	20 33	13 31	—	
6	F	Feast of St Nicholas	07:49	15:52	08 48	21 37	13 48	01 00	
7	Sa	Pearl Harbour 1941	07:51	15:52	09 50	22 32	14 05	02 07	Mild and wet at the start with much colder and windier conditions following for much of the month. Typically gale-prone at the close following a temporary calm, mild interval over Christmas.
8	Su	Sammy Davies Jnr b. 1925	07:52	15:52	10 44	23 20	14 22	03 14	
9	M	YMCA op. 1851	07:53	15:51	11 31	—	14 42	04 24	
10	Tu	Human Rights Day	07:54	15:51	00 02	12 14	15 07	05 35	
11	W	Edward VIII abdication 1936	07:55	15:51	00 41	12 54	15 37	16 47	
12	Th	Frank Sinatra b. 1915	07:56	15:51	01 19	13 34	16 16	07 59	
13	F	3-day week begins 1973	07:57	15:51	01 57	14 14	17 06	09 05	
14	Sa	Prince Albert d. 1861	07:58	15:51	02 35	14 56	18 08	10 03	
15	Su	Emperor Nero b. 37AD	07:59	15:51	03 16	15 40	19 20	10 50	
16	M	Jane Austen b. 1775	08:00	15:51	03 59	16 27	20 39	11 27	
17	Tu	Vogue first edition 1892	08:00	15:51	04 45	17 18	21 59	11 57	
18	W	First Thanksgiving 1777	08:01	15:52	05 36	18 16	23 20	12 21	
19	Th	Henry II crowned 1154	08:02	15:52	06 34	19 21	—	12 43	
20	F	Jenny Agutter b. 1952	08:02	15:52	07 39	20 29	00 41	13 03	
21	Sa	Benjamin Disraeli b. 1804	08:03	15:53	08 48	21 36	02 01	13 24	
22	Su	Winter solstice (04 19)	08:04	15:53	09 54	22 38	03 21	13 46	
23	M	Carol Ann Duffy b. 1955	08:04	15:54	10 55	23 33	04 41	14 13	
24	Tu	Christmas Eve	08:04	15:54	11 51	—	05 59	14 45	
25	W	Christmas Day	08:05	15:55	00 23	12 42	07 12	15 24	
26	Th	Annular eclipse (05 17)	08:05	15:56	01 09	13 29	08 18	16 13	
27	F	Louis Pasteur b. 1822	08:05	15:57	01 52	14 15	09 12	17 11	
28	Sa	Roy Hattersley b. 1932	08:06	15:57	02 34	14 58	09 56	18 15	
29	Su	Becket murdered 1170	08:06	15:58	03 15	15 41	10 29	19 23	
30	M	Rudyard Kipling b. 1865	08:06	15:59	03 55	16 23	10 56	20 31	
31	Tu	New Year's Eve/Hogmanay	08:06	16:00	04 36	17 06	11 18	21 38	

MOON'S PHASES DECEMBER 2019

			Days	Hours	Mins
☽	First Quarter		4	06	58
○	Full Moon		12	05	12
☾	Last Quarter		19	04	57
●	New Moon		26	05	13

All times on this page are GMT

PREDICTIONS

The Full Moon on 12 December is in Gemini on the eighth house cusp. Mars is rising at London indicating arguments over the national state of personal debt, mortgages, tax-relief and the costs of social care. Arguments between the needs of young people and the elderly will not be resolved. There is a renewed focus on high-tech communication with massive new investment in automated transport systems but also regulation of the web and attempts to ban mobile phones from schools. The Korean Peninsular is the global flashpoint, and Japan should take the lead in preventing conflict.

The New Moon on 26 December is an eclipse in Capricorn. This is a key moment to reset the global world order to move away from confrontation and back to co-operation, and emphasise international prosperity rather than national interests. Political change focuses on south-west Africa. Angola is booming thanks to its natural resources, but becomes the focus of investigations into multinational corporate crime. In south-east Asia, Indonesia becomes the focus for a new set of financial deals designed to lure business away from the West. We end the year on a positive note with widespread agreement that peace is a better way forward than war.

At Chepstow, the *Welsh National* may be won by a 5-year-old carrying 10st 10lb, whilst in the *King George VI Chase* at Kempton a 6-year-old may win, especially as a rapidly-rising second favourite.

48

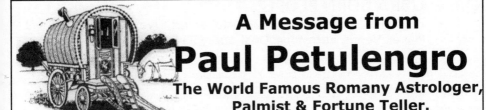

A Message from
Paul Petulengro
The World Famous Romany Astrologer, Palmist & Fortune Teller.

© Copyright Paul Petulengro 1937-2016

A True Born Gypsy with a Gift that will Astound You!

Need A Little Help?

- **Going through difficult times?**
- **Life holding you back?**
- **In search of a better, brighter future?**

If your Answer is YES to any one of the above Then Contact me TODAY without delay. Let me Help guide you down that Mysterious Path Ahead we call the FUTURE As I have thousands of others worldwide over the past 55 years.

Send NO Money, Just your

Full Name, Address and Birth Date (Block Capitals)

And I will send you your own **FREE 'Romany STARscope'** together with details of how I can make your Predictions and Directions for the **FULL** Twelve months ahead, a very successful **Lucky Numbers System** and YOUR very own **Golden Helping Hand** to the Future. Write **NOW,** remember you have nothing to lose but **everything** to gain.

Paul Petulengro
Casa Almendra
Las Pilas, LOJA 18314
Granada, SPAIN

© Copyright Paul Petulengro 1937 - 2016

LIBRA BORN PEOPLE
Birthdays: 24 September to 23 October inclusive
Planet: Venus. Birthstone: Opal. Lucky day: Friday

Keynote for the Year: *What happens at home this year may be hard work and not meet with expectations, but socially there are new opportunities for growth and the prospect of a new idea.*

JANUARY: MAIN TRENDS: 1–2 A secure period when you can make good progress towards your career and social goals. **6–7** The responsibilities of career and family may weigh heavily on you. Lift your spirits by taking time out to indulge in some nostalgia with someone close. **21–22** A personal matter may need delicate handling – don't take anything for granted, especially with your partner. **KEY DATES: HIGHS 4–5** You're likely to get more of your own way around this time – you only have to ask! **LOWS 19–20** Progress on the whole may be sluggish. Put major issues to one side, as there may be no easy solution to a problem.

FEBRUARY: MAIN TRENDS: 3–4 You may think you have the best advice for friends and colleagues but try to accept that this is a matter of opinion. **10–11** A favourable time for problem solving, getting to the root of personal issues and talking things over. **18–19** Trends suggest that you may need to make critical decisions that have far-reaching implications for your work. You may even be involved in something secretive! **KEY DATES: HIGHS 22–23** Trust your hunches if you need to take a risk and you may find things go your way. **LOWS 9–10** This is a low period so don't try too hard to get on but take some rest instead.

MARCH: MAIN TRENDS: 1–3 This trend should find you in the best of company and elicit much in the way of goodwill and generosity. A good time for romantic or pleasurable outings. **19–20** Some good ideas are in the air; trends highlight communication so there should be some useful information coming your way. **26–27** Domestic affairs should help to bring out the best in you as your nearest and dearest demonstrate a deeper understanding of personal matters. **KEY DATES: HIGHS 21–22** Decisions taken now should prove very successful – an excellent opportunity for short-term advancement. **LOWS 8–9** Life might seem a chore right now, but look at it as a time to reap what you've sown.

APRIL: MAIN TRENDS: 15–16 Romantic encounters may be eventful and exciting and as long as you can hog the limelight, you will be feeling fine! **20–21** You can pave the way for financial success under this influence that assists you to achieve your economic goals and attain security. **22–23** Potentially a 'red letter day' for your aims and objectives; capitalise on any new opportunity. **KEY DATES: HIGHS 17–18** An energising time when you'll probably go for what you want with zest – don't be afraid to take chances. **LOWS 4–5** You will need to work hard for what you want today, and perhaps get by with limited resources.

MAY: MAIN TRENDS: 6–7 You have what it takes to occupy a high profile position where charisma and personal identity play a prime role. **17–18** Money matters should now be stable which may give you the chance to bring a certain project to a successful conclusion. **20–21** New opportunities may arise at work, perhaps involving innovations or inventive ideas. You can make your own luck. **KEY DATES: HIGHS 15–16** An element of good fortune lends a hand to certain matters so press on with it! **LOWS 1–3; 29–30** Don't expect everything to run smoothly, and make plenty of time for indulgence and rest.

JUNE: MAIN TRENDS: 4–5 The further your travels take you the better; what you experience should be inspirational and open your eyes to short-term possibilities. **9–10** A great period to broaden your horizons and take a step in a completely new direction. **21–22** The mood for creative change creeps into a personal relationship and your partner should recognise this as well as you. **KEY DATES: HIGHS 11–12** Time to get busy during this important time for decision making. **LOWS 25–26** Resist any temptation to be vague in your communication with others, and certainly to be deceptive or evasive!

JULY: MAIN TRENDS: 3–4 You may have intuitive ideas that are creative and original – and you may even meet and make friends with other original thinkers. **25–26** Short trips and unexpected, exciting news may give you a greater sense of independence. Favourable professional trends may assist you to change the boss's mind about something. **28–29** A friendship may prove tiresome in certain ways, one of which is resurgence of certain disputes. Perhaps you need to clear the air with someone. **KEY DATES: HIGHS 8–9** Right now, with energy to spare, you should get a lot done – so go for it! **LOWS 22–24** Practical progress may be hampered by the need to spend time solving problems.

AUGUST: MAIN TRENDS: 11–12 You may have to dig in your heels over a personal dispute. This may even leave you rather unpopular – but a little attention can put things right. **17–18** You may see new opportunities for speedy progress at work and there may even be a breakthrough of some kind, one that you've been waiting for. **23–24** Exploit all possibilities to the full, whether personal whims or professional duties. **KEY DATES: HIGHS 5–6** An advantageous period all round, the 'green light' is on! **LOWS 19–21** Don't allow a matter from the past to distract you from current issues.

SEPTEMBER: MAIN TRENDS: 13–14 Dynamism and determination are your strengths when it comes to career ambitions. Be ready to overcome any obstacle in your pursuit of success. **17–18** You may be reluctant to deal with practical obligations but press on, as things may not be as they appear. **23–24** Work may be challenging, and you may have to deal with unsympathetic superiors. Don't be afraid to strike out on your own if the time is right. **KEY DATES: HIGHS 1–2; 28–29** Where progress is to be made an optimistic air should prevail. **LOWS 15–16** Keep to the tried-and-tested path and avoid any obstacles, especially in the workplace.

OCTOBER: MAIN TRENDS: 3–4 Go for anything that helps to broaden your world, in particular travel, cultural activities or intellectual pursuits. Also a good time to look for a promotion, too. **8–9** A favourable trend that stimulates your capacity to attract new and interesting people from all walks of life. **23–24** This influence may create new opportunities to meet people socially and you may even attract a new love interest; be on the lookout for friendly faces. **KEY DATES: HIGHS 26–27** Major decisions made now can have a vital effect on your short-term future. **LOWS 12–14** Get on with your obligations at work, even if some of them are rather unexpected.

NOVEMBER: MAIN TRENDS: 1–2 Organize your life and strive to meet your essential obligations. Engaging in new projects or working with loved ones can bring favourable results. **19–20** Seize the chance to bring a plan of action to fruition, you have everything to gain. **26–27** Attention paid to joint business matters may reveal scope for highly rewarding and profitable improvements in the long term. **KEY DATES: HIGHS 22–24** Make the most of this progressive trend. A little sensible risk-taking may put you on a winning streak. **LOWS 8–10** Responsibilities keep you busy and you are challenged to keep day-to-day affairs on an even keel.

DECEMBER: MAIN TRENDS: 9–10 Get new professional endeavours underway and if there are any special favours required, now is the time to ask. **17–18** Friends, associates and work colleagues are generally co-operative and open to your ideas and overtures. **22–23** Emphasise your best points and simplify routines where you can. Opportunities may prove lucrative as your finances are positively highlighted. **KEY DATES: HIGHS 19–21** Don't be afraid to seek help from influential people – the bigger your ideas, the better. **LOWS 6–7** Don't overburden yourself with too many obligations and consider a current plan of action carefully.

SCORPIO BORN PEOPLE
Birthdays: 24 October to 22 November inclusive
Planets: Mars, Pluto. Birthstone: Topaz. Lucky day: Tuesday

Keynote for the Year: *You may find you're somewhat out of step with other people's ideas this year, but channel your energies into financial interests and the rewards may be considerable.*

JANUARY: MAIN TRENDS: 1–2 As the year begins you may need to make fundamental changes to your lifestyle. As you embark on fresh starts you can put an end to old situations. **5–6** You may need some self-restraint in your dealings with people socially – if strong views are aired openly they may need to be resolved with sensitivity. **20–21** Trends help you to move things along and improve communications, putting you firmly in the picture. **KEY DATES: HIGHS 27–29** Don't be afraid to take on life-changing decisions at this time. **LOWS 15–16** Try to keep a cool head if things go wrong or you hear something that confuses you.

FEBRUARY: MAIN TRENDS: 3–4 Influences suggest that close relationships may be disheartening and a heart-to-heart may be necessary if you are really to get through to the one you love. **9–10** Fresh starts are the order of the day as you have a positive frame of mind and a renewed sense of vigour. **18–19** This trend indicates a sharp wit, mental energy and a persuasive manner so put your silver tongue to excellent use. **KEY DATES: HIGHS 24–25** You can afford to be competitive in professional affairs and things should work out successfully. **LOWS 11–12** Setbacks are likely but you should still attend to any unfinished business.

MARCH: MAIN TRENDS: 1–3 Communications are favourably highlighted so look out for some interesting news. Enjoy the freedom to get to know a variety of acquaintances. **20–21** Powerful influences surround your personal finances – a potentially stable phase when you can make steady progress towards your goals. **26–27** Although you may be wary of the outcome of certain plans your caution may be unjustified. A loved one may help you to have faith. **KEY DATES: HIGHS 23–24** A favourable period for self-improvement when you may be luckier than expected. **LOWS 10–12** Trends suggest you may be suspicious, but give others the benefit of the doubt if you are not in possession of the facts.

APRIL: MAIN TRENDS: 17–18 The short-term prospects look good for your love life and you may feel like getting away from routines and out and about. Explore your creative side. **22–23** Your desire for new mind-broadening experiences continues unabated and trends now help you to get more from life, especially on a cultural level. **22–23** Planetary influences may bring about a yearning for the 'good old days'; a trip down memory lane should satisfy your sentimental side. **KEY DATES: HIGHS 20–21** Use your ambitious energy to get a new project rolling. **LOWS 7–8** Unfolding events may not be in your best interests; take care not to be susceptible to the influence of others.

MAY: MAIN TRENDS: 6–7 The planets point to a successful day professionally, where much should go your way with the support of superiors. **15–16** You should enjoy getting on with practical tasks and with a little ingenuity, plans on the drawing board should move ahead smoothly. **20–21** One of your best times of the month to relish spending with others and enjoying their company. **KEY DATES: HIGHS 17–18** An optimistic outlook makes a real difference now. Someone may do you an unexpected favour. **LOWS 4–5; 31** Keep a low profile and put big tasks aside for a while.

JUNE: MAIN TRENDS: 4–5 The planets give you the ability to charm others into doing things your way; in particular, getting the best from your partner seems to be your forte! **9–10** There may be opportunities for success at work so have confidence in what you are doing. **21–22** Travel is positively highlighted so set out to broaden your horizons with trips that are of cultural or intellectual interest. **KEY DATES: HIGHS 13–14** Keep your positive resolve focused on your higher purpose and long-term ambitions. **LOWS 1; 28–29** Practical achievements may be difficult to attain but don't allow boredom to push you into impulsive action.

JULY: MAIN TRENDS: 3–4 Socially and romantically your powers of attraction increase, and you show good, and creative, judgement in a major decision. **23–24** A favourable period for adventure, travel and anything to do with the outdoors but also a good time to improve your mind. **28–29** This appears to be a lucrative period for you. You should be in a stable position to set about planning for the future. **KEY DATES: HIGHS 10–11** A time to make excellent headway with your business and professional affairs. **LOWS 25–26** Concentrate on the job at hand and take steps to avoid unnecessary risks.

AUGUST: MAIN TRENDS: 11–12 Expect to make great progress at work – you have energy and ambition and the support of those in authority. **21–22** The positive trends at work continue as you accomplish much towards your objectives – rapidly and smoothly. **24–25** Your mind works fast now, so much so that others may be unable to keep up with you. But your quick thinking can be put to excellent use. **KEY DATES: HIGHS 7–8** Getting your own way with others is a major strength now. Use it! **LOWS 21–23** A temporary low patch; take things one thing at a time if you feel a little down.

SEPTEMBER: MAIN TRENDS: 13–14 You benefit from being forthcoming and assertive – it's a great time for any joint enterprises or business relationships. **15–16** Your sway and influence over life in general is not as powerful as you'd like, but this trend should give you superior intuition when it comes to figuring others out. **23–24** A rewarding phase and a good time to organise family and domestic affairs. You may benefit from events connected with the past. **KEY DATES: HIGHS 3–4** Intuitive and resourceful now, don't be afraid to back your hunches. **LOWS 17–19** You can't expect the best results from your efforts now, so shelve anything of great importance.

OCTOBER: MAIN TRENDS: 3–4 A good time for careful planning and tackling your responsibilities. Certain material plans ought to be doing rather nicely. **8–9** Challenging issues may result in conflict requiring fast action and great energy. Co-operation is needed with those in power and authority. **23–24** The beginning of an optimistic period when relationships prove pretty exciting. Alternatively, why not call up an old and dear friend? **KEY DATES: HIGHS 28–29** A perfect time to share experiences and insight with a trusted individual. **LOWS 15–16** Expect to feel some temporary anxiety because of circumstances beyond your control. This will pass.

NOVEMBER: MAIN TRENDS: 1–2 Let go of the reins of power and look within yourself; a more reflective view of life may benefit you. **22–23** Put some ideas to the test and use all your effort to make them work wonderfully; you should then be on the right path to your objectives. **26–27** At work you may be in a position of power and influence, if only because of your charming but incisive manner. **KEY DATES: HIGHS 24–25** New energy may now lead to considerable expansion in certain areas of your life. Time to go for it! **LOWS 11–12** Don't jump to conclusions about others – it may turn out to be a case of bad judgement.

DECEMBER: MAIN TRENDS: 11–12 You have what it takes to bring out the best in your partner, friends and loved ones right now – and this increases your popularity. **20–21** Joint financial dealings are favourably highlighted, with new opportunities for gain and support from those close to you. A time of consolidation. **22–23** Once more you get along splendidly with others, especially in teamwork situations, and may prove lucky in love and friendship, especially the latter. **KEY DATES: HIGHS 22–23** A great time to discuss new opportunities and joint plans with colleagues and partners. **LOWS 8–10** Beware of some 'upsets' to the smooth running of practical affairs.

SAGITTARIUS BORN PEOPLE
Birthdays: 23 November to 21 December inclusive
Planet: Jupiter. Birthstone: Turquoise. Lucky day: Thursday

Keynote for the Year: *Jupiter, the planet of growth and opportunity, passes through your sign this year, enabling you to put your dreams and schemes into action. Strike while the iron is hot!*

JANUARY: MAIN TRENDS: 5–6 This is a relaxed time when your loved ones put you at ease and you feel secure in the affection of your family. **7–8** Thoughts turn to business and you may be streets ahead of the competition. People in authority may give you their approval. **20–21** Meetings, appointments and discussions with others may lead to some interesting proposals. **KEY DATES: HIGHS 2–4; 30–31** Planetary trends indicate some sudden and unexpected changes in your daily life, most likely for the better. **LOWS 17–18** Though you like your independence, don't try to go it alone just now but instead enlist some help.

FEBRUARY: MAIN TRENDS: 3–4 Beware of rushing blindly into action without thinking – especially at work. **10–11** Co-operation with others is positively highlighted – things definitely go better in pairs, whatever you are doing. **18–19** Don't hide your light under the proverbial bushel. You may come up with creative new ideas that help life in unexpected ways – make sure you get them noticed. **KEY DATES: HIGHS 26–27** A progressive time of good ideas and all the support you need to get things moving. **LOWS 13–15** It is unrealistic to expect everything to run smoothly now. Take time to rest.

MARCH: MAIN TRENDS: 1–3 You're very good at focusing on other people's better qualities and find relationships with friends and colleagues to be supportive. A win-win situation. **20–21** Buckle down and get busy – put your boundless energy to good use at work. **28–29** You are inspirational and overflowing with ideas for all future plans, but particularly at work. **KEY DATES: HIGHS 25–27** You may need to assess the profitability of certain changes. Progress should not be long in coming, though. **LOWS 13–14** Expect the unexpected during this planetary low; you may feel a little out of tune with the world.

APRIL: MAIN TRENDS: 17–18 Your successful touch with others is emphasised and their warm response is to be expected. Everyone wants to be in your good books. **20–21** Focus on the practical side of life; get things organised and sort the wheat from the chaff. Unexpected material benefits may accrue. **24–25** Your love life may give you food for thought. A complete change of scenery may help your need for independence. **KEY DATES: HIGHS 22–23** Work as hard as possible and consolidate your recent achievements. **LOWS 9–10** If your progress in general is dragging its heels, take a break and don't push so hard.

MAY: MAIN TRENDS: 8–9 Whilst there seems to be much of interest going on in the social world don't fall behind with tasks that require immediate attention. **15–16** Although you can be very inventive in both your business and personal life, it may be a challenge to adapt to change. Trends suggest that you may enjoy a little nostalgia now. **22–23** You benefit greatly from being on the move so prioritise any travel plans or at least try to get out for a day. **KEY DATES: HIGHS 19–20** With Lady Luck onside, something ought to put a smile on your face. **LOWS 6–7** Play it safe for a while and ride out this planetary low patch.

JUNE: MAIN TRENDS: 5–6 Teamwork should be extremely enjoyable right now. You like to stand out in the crowd and thrive on group situations as these show your popularity. **9–10** Trends indicate that you will now want to get to the heart of a matter and won't be satisfied with a superficial answer. **21–22** Slow things down and take a broader view of life; you can benefit from an 'anything goes' attitude and less desire for personal gain. **KEY DATES: HIGHS 15–17** A beneficial trend when you may double your luck in certain initiatives. **LOWS 2–4; 30** If it becomes obvious that certain adjustments are needed in a practical matter, go with it.

JULY: MAIN TRENDS: 3–4 An influx of important new ideas and information, even on the grapevine, put you in the know in certain areas. You may also gain from long-distance travel. **23–24** Expect a little good fortune at home. With support from your family you may enjoy some time spent re-living the past. **29–30** With a flair for financial dealings you can pave the way for your economic goals. **KEY DATES: HIGHS 13–14** The potential for success is strong and you are now pushing forward like never before. **LOWS 1; 27–28** Take care not to overestimate your abilities and strengths, and prepare for some setbacks.

AUGUST: MAIN TRENDS: 11–12 Your personality receives a planetary boost so you may want to take the starring role, especially socially and with your partner. **21–22** Thoughts turn to improvements, whether to your surroundings or your life; there is a drive to get to the bottom of things. **22–23** The domestic scene looks busy as trends highlight home and family matters. A great time for entertaining friends. **KEY DATES: HIGHS 9–10** With vitality and enthusiasm you might just make a great impact on someone. **LOWS 24–25** If you can't get what you want, stay calm and accept a little disappointment.

SEPTEMBER: MAIN TRENDS: 13–14 The emphasis is on fun as this planetary influence stimulates your romantic side. You could do little better than being among friends in a social setting. **15–16** Although you can be ingenious and forward-looking, certain big ideas may be less valuable than you had imagined. **23–24** It shouldn't be too hard to find a warm welcome socially as trends highlight your ability to attract good company. There may be new acquaintances on the horizon. **KEY DATES: HIGHS 5–6** A lucky trend which favours tackling big tasks. **LOWS 20–21** Some plans may be upset but this is part of the temporary low phase so try to accept it with grace.

OCTOBER: MAIN TRENDS: 5–6 Meetings with others may inspire some new ideas – the trouble is you may be not be listening! Don't be so focused on getting your point across that you fail to hear others. **8–9** A partnership may prove lucky for you in some way. Meet up with friends, whether old or new. **23–24** Trends lend you an expansive, forward-looking approach; a change of scene helps you to make the most of this. **KEY DATES: HIGHS 2–4; 3–31** A word in the right ear may hasten your progress. Those who hesitate finish last! **LOWS 17–18** A good deal of patience is needed to cope with the business of the day.

NOVEMBER: MAIN TRENDS: 1–2 Ring the changes in a family plan to avoid things becoming too samey. News at work may lead to a change of direction. **22–23** Knuckle down to your obligations even if your desire for fun makes them feel onerous. **28–29** A favourable time for your love life – make this a special day for you and your partner, especially if there are new interests on the horizon. **KEY DATES: HIGHS 26–27** Lady Luck smiles on you during this pleasant phase. **LOWS 13–15** Trends indicate a mistake made through oversight or overconfidence. Check everything carefully to avoid falling into this trap.

DECEMBER: MAIN TRENDS: 9–10 Be wary of someone trying to manipulate your ideas; make up your own mind and go with your instincts. **20–21** Your social life keeps you smiling, and you may also learn something from it if you keep your eyes open. **22–23** Matters of the heart have a lot going for them be beware if you see new romance on the horizon, you may get more than you bargained for! **KEY DATES: HIGHS 24–25** A key phase of the month, which suggests a lucky and happy Christmas. **LOWS 11–12** Time constraints may leave little space for fun and leisure. A social plan may have to be rearranged.

CAPRICORN BORN PEOPLE
Birthdays: 22 December to 20 January inclusive
Planet: Saturn. Birthstone: Garnet. Lucky day: Saturday

Keynote for the Year: *Your ruling planet, Saturn, is at home in your sign now: consolidate and secure are the watchwords. A time of consequences when your actions begin to yield real results.*

JANUARY: MAIN TRENDS: 1–2 You will enjoy getting back to work in the New Year and getting your plans underway. Expect to be the big boss you like to be! **5–6** Socially speaking, this may be a day filled with fun. A friend may be the source of reward or some significant information. **21–22** An uplifting and interesting period for your domestic affairs. An influx of visitors may lead you to seek some privacy, though. **KEY DATES: HIGHS 5–6** Don't hesitate to make requests of others, especially superiors work. **LOWS 19–20** Take time to rethink a recent project and pay attention to the smaller details.

FEBRUARY: MAIN TRENDS: 3–4 Your most fulfilling moments come from private matters now. An issue from the past may help you put some of the present in perspective. **10–11** A personal matter arises at home and it seems that the way through is clear if you are prepared to discuss things honestly. **18–19** The best thing one can say about work right now is that new friendships and social gatherings are likely! This should not affect your work itself, though. **KEY DATES: HIGHS 1–2; 28** Put new ideas and schemes into operation without further ado! **LOWS 16–17** A quiet phase when rest and relaxation are called for.

MARCH: MAIN TRENDS: 3–4 Your opinions won't appeal to everyone, although some will no doubt admire your tough talking in situations that really require it. **20–21** The breath of fresh air from this influence enlivens your relationships and social life – be open to new, even radical, ideas. **26–27** Professionally, things ought to go with a swing so take care not to play it too safe. Someone in authority may prove influential. **KEY DATES: HIGHS 1–2; 28–29** With optimism and confidence in your abilities, strike out for what you want. **LOWS 15–16** Be lucid in your communications with associates to avoid confusion.

APRIL: MAIN TRENDS: 17–18 You may now be in a favourable position to get ahead with practical matters, and you needn't focus only on essentials. **20–21** Progress at work should be easy to make as you have just about all the support you need – the more ambitious you are now, the better. **22–23** You'll probably want to maintain a high profile and you should – there may be plenty of opportunities to enjoy the attentions of others. **KEY DATES: HIGHS 24–25** Now you should be in control at work so tempt fate a little while the planets are on your side. **LOWS 11–12** Accept that delays are inevitable during the monthly low patch.

MAY: MAIN TRENDS: 6–7 Trends increase your ego: watch out world! You may have a tendency to take a dominant role in relationships to make sure everything is as you like it. **15–16** A far more helpful influence work-wise when it should be easier to get things into better order. Don't miss any opportunity to take a step further up the ladder. **19–20** Socially this should be a very fulfilling period as friendly encounters are warm and affectionate. Your love life may see promising new developments. **KEY DATES: HIGHS 21–23** Put a little faith in Lady Luck, but always listen to your instincts. **LOWS 8–9** An issue at work might be frustrating – prepare to grit your teeth and cut your losses.

JUNE: MAIN TRENDS: 3–4 A talk with a friend or colleague may be inspirational; put their practical advice to good use. **9–10** You intend to be noticed but don't overdo it. The need to assert yourself shouldn't override other more fundamental considerations. **21–22** Personal relationships should be warm and intimate under this influence, and it's an excellent time to talk over emotional issues and bare your soul. **KEY DATES: HIGHS 18–19** With superior organisational skills and a lot of energy you can look forward to satisfactory results. **LOWS 5–6** Personal success may be difficult to achieve, so take some time out.

JULY: MAIN TRENDS: 4–5 You enjoy being 'in the know' as the pace of life steps up. Information received now may be just the kind you have been seeking, so put it to good use. **23–24** Trends highlighting your career indicate that you can make the most of recent circumstances, whether through invaluable help or smooth progress, you should be on a winning streak. **27–28** A lively time for get-togethers with friends. **KEY DATES: HIGHS 15–16** Act on new opportunities and you should be on a winning streak at work. **LOWS 2–3; 29–31** What you learn from a work colleague may demonstrate how you have been getting things wrong.

AUGUST: MAIN TRENDS: 13–14 Various pressures from the outside world should lessen and the pace become more relaxed. A domestic issue may help to cheer you up as well. **21–22** The need for fun and to enjoy the lighter side of life is paramount, and there ought to be plenty of opportunity to do so right now. **23–24** A successful time for personal relationships as trends boost your mood. Your charisma is in plentiful supply! **KEY DATES: HIGHS 11–12** There is no time like the present under these extremely favourable trends for Capricorn – go for it! **LOWS 26–27** Shelve certain plans and wind down big jobs if possible; instead attend to simpler unfinished business.

SEPTEMBER: MAIN TRENDS: 13–14 Spend some time at the drawing board, working on your plans before you put them into action. **15–16** Events taking place in groups should work out nicely for you. Working together as a team has many advantages, whether personally or at work. **24–25** An intellectual exchange may be significant as you broaden your horizons. A beneficial time for taking up new studies. **KEY DATES: HIGHS 7–9** Exploit every opportunity for financial gain now. **LOWS 22–23** Adopt a cautious and realistic attitude to your affairs, especially if others seem determined to cause problems.

OCTOBER: MAIN TRENDS: 3–4 Relationships are positively highlighted but getting your own way with others is largely a matter of charm right now, no matter who they are. **8–9** Professional talks and deals may need a rethink, but you may receive new support for your long-term plans. **23–24** Good things continue to happen professionally – it's an auspicious time for seeking promotion as well as any travel related to your job. **KEY DATES: HIGHS 5–7** The best time to make a fresh start or take a little chance. **LOWS 20–21** Accept the inevitability of some setbacks at this time.

NOVEMBER: MAIN TRENDS: 3–4 Seek out an old friend or family member you haven't seen in a long time and relive the good old days. **22–23** This influence is all about the need for self-reliance, so keep on top of practical affairs even if you have fewer resources than usual. **26–27** Personal relationships may contain more than an element of drama as certain feelings become apparent. But something needs sorting out here. **KEY DATES: HIGHS 1–2; 29–30** If you are prepared to take a measured risk then you could reap some favourable results, at home or at work. **LOWS 16–17** Deal with emotional issues from the past before moving ahead.

DECEMBER: MAIN TRENDS: 9–10 A potentially pressurised period when you may need to work through personal changes; abandon anything that has run its course. **20–21** Get out and about and look forward to an exciting and pleasurable period of socialising or romance. **22–23** Your social life is likely to be running more or less as you'd wish and trends bring out your best qualities. **KEY DATES: HIGHS 26–27** There is little reason why social plans should not go your way so put plans into action. **LOWS 13–14** Take time to relax while your energies are low.

AQUARIUS BORN PEOPLE
Birthdays: 21 January to 19 February inclusive
Planets: Saturn, Uranus. Birthstone: Amethyst. Lucky day: Saturday

Keynote for the Year: *Your social circle may extend without any effort from you this year, and friendships can really change your life. But issues from the past may need serious attention.*

JANUARY: MAIN TRENDS: 1–2 The year may begin with the need to deal with a difficult relationship. Try to work out problems with an intimate chat. **5–6** A favourable time to negotiate agreements. Your ideas may be of tremendous help to a colleague or friend. **19–20** Find something mentally stimulating to do: travel or an outing of cultural interest may be enlightening. **KEY DATES: HIGHS 7–9** A physical and mental peak when your judgement and timing is impeccable. **LOWS 21–22** Put big plans to one side and get on with something easier during the low part of the month.

FEBRUARY: MAIN TRENDS: 2–3 Things come together quite nicely at work, whether fresh starts or completing projects. Your energy stands you in good stead and your accomplishments should be satisfactory. **10–11** An exchange of views could be productive now; you learn something new every day and this period proves it. Travel is also favourably highlighted. **20–21** A professionally demanding period, but you should be buoyed up by beneficial results. Don't overlook the smallest chance of advancement. **KEY DATES: HIGHS 4–5** A friend may do you a surprising favour at work. **LOWS 18–19** Beware that unnecessary risks may lead to setbacks.

MARCH: MAIN TRENDS: 5–6 You are on a roll with your financial or professional decisions and it seems that certain material goals are now easily attainable. **20–21** You are highly personable now which means that you come across well and consequently others take notice of you. **26–27** You bring out the best in others and demonstrate that the secret of social popularity is getting others to feel good about themselves. **KEY DATES: HIGHS 3–4; 30–31** Under auspicious trends your powers should be in the ascendant. **LOWS 17–18** Prepare for the fact that some practical setbacks may lead to rather long delays.

APRIL: MAIN TRENDS: 17–18 Abandon whatever isn't working and look at starting again – but not until you have cleared out any clutter in your life. **20–21** A time of change and re-evaluation; in particular, a financial issue may need special attention. Don't make personal security the main focus of your thoughts right now. **22–23** You'll be the life and soul of the party so concentrate of leisure and pleasure; you are highly entertaining company. **KEY DATES: HIGHS 1; 26–27** A peak period with much opportunity for success – your decisions and aims are on target. **LOWS 13–14** The monthly planetary lull signifies that it's time to slow things down for a day or so.

MAY: MAIN TRENDS: 6–7 Your personal influence over day-to-day matters may be less than you'd expected. If you are open and receptive to new ideas this may help things. **15–16** Your social life improves, especially as trends suggest you may meet some interesting newcomers. **20–21** Indulge in some pleasant nostalgia and look to events from the past to give you ease and bring you comfort in your surroundings. **KEY DATES: HIGHS 24–25** A progressive time when any recent delays disappear. **LOWS 11–12** Your material progress may be less encouraging than you would like, and it seems you need all the help you can get.

JUNE: MAIN TRENDS: 4–5 A go-getting period but nevertheless one in which you should be cautious about finances. Avoid false optimism regarding new monetary deals or investments. **9–10** A little good news may come your way as planetary influences put you in touch with the stream of significant information. **22–23** An uplifting time intellectually; someone may open your eyes a little more to certain facts of life and you seem to be on a learning curve. **KEY DATES: HIGHS 20–21** Enjoy ploughing your efforts into your career to reap the rewards. **LOWS 7–8** Mistakes made now may be due to unrealistic thinking so keep both feet on the ground.

JULY MAIN TRENDS: 2–3 Revisiting past ideas may prove worthwhile, but keep an open mind about professional changes coming your way. **23–24** A busy time at work when you may need to be organised, but don't get so wrapped up that you miss important news. **28–29** Social get-togethers may prove interesting and you may be on a winning streak when it comes to refreshing intellectual experiences. **KEY DATES: HIGHS 17–19** It should be easy to call in a favour if you are trying to get new projects off the ground. **LOWS 4–5** You may need to make your own luck, especially if loved ones are difficult to handle.

AUGUST: MAIN TRENDS: 11–12 Moves made in the area of finances may see concrete results. Your economic situation is positively highlighted which fosters the right environment for growth. **21–22** A situation involving a friend may lead to new scope for new romance. A fine period for all kinds of relationship. **23–24** It seems that people will show you their generous side and this may prove very helpful. Work should be running smoothly. **KEY DATES: HIGHS 14–15** This may prove to be one of the luckiest times of the month for a little risk-taking. **LOWS 1–2; 28–29** Keep your patience and avoid needless disputes at home.

SEPTEMBER: MAIN TRENDS: 13–14 The right time for simple pleasures and enjoying the lighter side of life. A sudden reversal may well turn out to be a blessing. **15–16** Practical matters should be going your way but you may need to attend to the fine details. **26–27** Enjoy some entertainment now; this is just the right environment to make new friends. **KEY DATES: HIGHS 10–11** Trends highlight the chance of a change of career or perhaps a promotion. All serious enterprises are favoured. **LOWS 24–25** Accept that there may be no easy solution to a problem, no matter how hard you try.

OCTOBER: MAIN TRENDS: 3–4 You could be in great demand at work but it is in social interactions that the day may take an interesting turn. **10–11** A relaxing time when you can rest and indulge yourself in life's little pleasures, especially in the company of close family. **24–25** Trends assist your problem-solving abilities so you are now ready to grasp the nettle and tackle any issue. Remember to do so with sensitivity if you are dealing with a personal issue. **KEY DATES: HIGHS 7–9** An element of luck may help just about any endeavour. **LOWS 22–23** Although obstacles at work may be frustrating, getting emotional is not the solution.

NOVEMBER: MAIN TRENDS: 1–2 Trends help to make the domestic atmosphere happy at home; use this mood to engineer positive changes in your personal life. **22–23** Make the most of this period of good company and happy social occasions. Events in your love life seem almost tailor-made for you! **26–27** Taking on too many commitments could prove to be a big mistake now. Perhaps what you need is time to reenergise. **KEY DATES: HIGHS 3–5** With a little luck and some creative thinking you should make progress today. **LOWS 18–19** Keep a low profile, take it easy and ride out this quiet phase.

DECEMBER: MAIN TRENDS: 9–10 You work well as part of a team. You enjoy playing to a captive audience and want to stand out from the crowd. **20–21** Taking your place in the limelight is no trouble for you now – expect some positive results from the business of the day and to be able to make a big impact on someone important. **22–23** You could make a good impression on someone and there should be little to hold up your ambitions. **KEY DATES: HIGHS 1–2; 28–30** The need for freedom is strong, as is your desire to have things your own way. This need not be a bad thing, though. **LOWS 15–16** This is the perfect time to take a step back and reflect on life.

PISCES BORN PEOPLE
Birthdays: 20 February to 20 March inclusive
Planets: Jupiter, Neptune. Birthstone: Bloodstone. Lucky day: Thursday

Keynote for the Year: *Professional affairs may offer you significant opportunities to advance in the next twelve months as you take a more independent attitude to life in general.*

JANUARY: MAIN TRENDS: 1–2 Day-to-day life may feel full of complex issues, but it will be good to resolve long-standing problems and clear something from your life if necessary. **5–6** Expect to feel a curiosity about the unknown and to have the drive to seek out answers. As this is a good period for broadening personal horizons, it's the perfect time for this quest. **20–21** Your social life is looking good during this period and you may enjoy a feeling of usefulness. **KEY DATES: HIGHS 10–11** Put your luck to the test during this 'green light' period when things go your way. **LOWS 23–24** Be honest and open and don't allow petty issues to overwhelm you now.

FEBRUARY: MAIN TRENDS: 3–4 Your mind can't help turning to thoughts of business, even when you are away from work. Put your ideas to practical use when the time is right. **10–11** Dealing with those in a position of authority should be made easy by the right support now. You might be able to call the shots in a work situation. **18–19** This influence places a powerful focus on close relationships and makes them secure and rewarding. This mood may rub off on financial relationships, too! **KEY DATES: HIGHS 6–8** Think outside the box today and do someone a favour if they need it. **LOWS 20–21** Your partner should rally round if your spirits are low.

MARCH: MAIN TRENDS: 1–3 Trends benefit all sorts of partnerships so don't struggle on alone. There may be promising new social encounters. **21–22** Self-determination is the way to success, but avoid the usual pitfalls and keep to tried-and-tested methods. **26–27** Accept the challenge to refresh any elements of your life that aren't working out during this go-ahead period. **KEY DATES: HIGHS 19–20** Approach someone influential with your problem and you may be surprised at how willing they are to help. **LOWS 5–7** Beware – a pressing matter may cloud your judgement in decision-making.

APRIL: MAIN TRENDS: 17–18 A very rewarding time at home as your partner conspires to make life comfortable. Reliving the good old days was never so good! **20–21** A successful time for your love life and your ego is boosted as well; let your personality shine and make an impact on others. **22–23** The pace of life may have stepped up and trends suggest you'll gain from many diverse interests. Conversations with others may leave them impressed. **KEY DATES: HIGHS 2–3; 29–30** The message during these times is: expect the best from life and you may just get it! **LOWS 15–16** Recognise the fact that responsibility must now take priority over recreation.

MAY: MAIN TRENDS: 6–7 Keep your eyes and ears open for any new information coming your way as you may learn something significant. **15–16** You might like to try a variety of tasks – push ahead at work and rise to the challenge, even if it means risking your popularity. **20–21** Professional developments may really be going places, but remember to keep a grip on reality and don't push things too far. **KEY DATES: HIGHS 26–28** You have energy to deal with any problem so get started as soon as possible. **LOWS 13–14** You enjoy organising people and your heart may be in the right place, but will everyone appreciate your help?

JUNE: MAIN TRENDS: 4–5 A new phase that points to good things happening in the home. Enjoy getting the best from loved ones and your nearest and dearest. **11–12** You may feel the urge to break out of monotonous patterns and pressures may force you to re-evaluate your situation. **21–22** You may help friends just by listening to their problems, but take care not to become caught up in negativity from the past. **KEY DATES: HIGHS 23–24** Complete any pressing projects at work – they might bring considerable success. **LOWS 9–10** Your energy may be in short supply, but you should still avoid pessimism or falling into the 'grass is greener' trap.

JULY: MAIN TRENDS: 3–4 Trends give a thrust towards self-determination, power and effectiveness – you probably feel you can take on the world right now. **23–24** A vibrant social mood colours this period when you will attract support and affection, especially in your private life. **28–29** The good things of life may come to you quite easily and you get what you need, just when you need it. **KEY DATES: HIGHS 20–21** A potentially lucky period when you have boundless get-up-and-go – make an early start. **LOWS 6–7** Keep to the tried-and-tested path and adjust any plans as necessary.

AUGUST: MAIN TRENDS: 11–12 There should be forces around you now that make work and practical matters far more rewarding. **21–22** Any complications are likely to come from your relationships – loved ones may need careful handling. **23–24** Making financial profit may come as second nature now as you enjoy growth and success in many areas. Slow and steady is the way forward though, with an eye to security. **KEY DATES: HIGHS 16–17** If you instinctively feel you are making the right moves it's likely you are, so keep on going! **LOWS 3–4; 30–31** Know when to quit or you'll end up losing more than you've gained.

SEPTEMBER: MAIN TRENDS: 11–12 Trust your intuition – this is a very good time for problem solving or for any research. **15–16** You need privacy and time to meditate on what you want from life in the long run. Trends suggest that you will want to spend time in quiet contemplation. **23–24** The spirit of togetherness brings happiness to your dealings with others. New faces may appear out of the woodwork. **KEY DATES: HIGHS 13–14** The accent is on romance and fun. Lady Luck may smile brightly on you during this phase. **LOWS 26–27** Put ambitions on the back burner and take a more reflective view of life for a day or so.

OCTOBER: MAIN TRENDS: 3–4 Your self-confidence helps you to achieve your goals and ambitions. Romantic relationships should be harmonious. **8–9** If you are feeling at ease with yourself, enjoy the mood and spend time with those close to you. **22–23** At the peak of your popularity, you may have to pick and choose from social invitations. **KEY DATES: HIGHS 10–11** A little optimism takes you a very long way right now. **LOWS 24–25** If a major plan of action hits a stumbling block, consider whether it is worth continuing.

NOVEMBER: MAIN TRENDS: 1–2 Broaden your view of life; travel and intellectual pastimes do you the power of good. **22–23** Keep busy, especially at work, and you should be out in front and well ahead of the competition. **26–27** Although your instincts may tell you to look ahead at the bigger picture, trends suggest that you should set your sights much lower – certainly don't go full steam ahead without adequate preparation. **KEY DATES: HIGHS 6–7** Luck is with you now so do as you please! **LOWS 20–21** A sluggish period when life may feel like a let down. Keep your demands of others to a minimum.

DECEMBER: MAIN TRENDS: 9–10 Your self-confidence rises so use this phase to take the initiative in your love life. **20–21** In a contrast to earlier in the month, you may now feel the need to withdraw, be alone and think things over. Don't be put upon by others. **22–23** Pressures from the outside world may lessen and thoughts turn to contentment in domestic relationships. Resolve a contentious issue, if necessary. **KEY DATES: HIGHS 3–4; 31** Trends aid your decision-making abilities so follow your heart and take a little chance if there is something you have been wanting to do that feels right. **LOWS 17–18** A complete break is called for – get two early nights!

Astrological Signs on the Cusp

If you were born two or three days either side of the change from one zodiac sign to the next, you were born 'on the cusp' and your astrological make-up is influenced by the adjacent sign. For more detail, look for the *Old Moore's Horoscope and Astral Diary* for your star sign in bookshops or at www.foulsham.com.

Pisces **Aries** Taurus	While still an ambitious Aries, you have emotional sensitivity and concern for others and are a good listener. This is a juxtaposition of opposites that can work in your favour.
	Less forceful than ambitious Aries, you may have a quieter aspect to your nature and find contentment in your tasteful home surrounded by a few close friends.
Aries **Taurus** Gemini	More of a go-getter, less patient and more forthright than steadfast Taurus, you could be inclined to be bossy as you have the Bull's determination overlaid with Aries' active energy.
	A mischievous Gemini streak lightens patient and reliable Taurus, and makes you easy-going and less inclined to take yourself too seriously, while still energetic and creative.
Taurus **Gemini** Cancer	Quieter than chatty Gemini, you benefit from being steadier and more determined, less mercurial and with a stronger ability to persevere both at work and in your relationships.
	Sensitive Cancer brings you the tendency to be less confident but more steadfast, emotional and considerate than intellectual Gemini, attached to home but enjoying travel.
Gemini **Cancer** Leo	Cancer's emotional sensitivity benefits from Gemini's confidence while losing its own fierce loyalty, so you are more inclined to speak your mind and show a brash, capable exterior.
	More outspoken than a typical Cancer but touched by the sunny Leo disposition that makes you outgoing for this sign, and more of an idealist who enjoys company and variety.
Cancer **Leo** Virgo	Slower than strong Leo but still cheerful, you are sensitive and able to compromise, although it may be difficult to predict which side of your nature will come to the fore.
	A complex combination – positive, outgoing Leo meets quiet, contemplative and rather intense Virgo. This partnership creates a basically friendly individual inclined to worry more than is good.
Leo **Virgo** Libra	Leo lightens intense Virgo, who is inclined to take itself too seriously, adding more self-confidence and popularity but supporting the tendency to work hard to achieve objectives.
	A good combination, because Virgo can be too intense and Libra rather flighty so this results in an intelligent and thoughtful person who is also practical and reliable.
Virgo **Libra** Scorpio	With Libra's practical and capable nature comes an increased drive and potential for success; an inspiring person with a better than the usual Libran capacity to listen to others.
	Less practical and more emotional than a typical Libra, you are nonetheless a responsible and caring individual with some Scorpio confidence to add to your pragmatic nature.
Libra **Scorpio** Sagittarius	While Libra seeks popularity, Scorpio speaks his mind, so you may enjoy the Libran diplomacy Scorpio lacks, or find that your outspokenness interferes with your popularity.
	A natural director of others, Scorpio loves to be in charge, is morally certain and determined, while Sagittarius brings you a witty and more intuitive personality.
Scorpio **Sagittarius** Capricorn	A well-liked combination, a touch of Scorpio makes you more contemplative and sensitive to others than a typical Sagittarius, while still enjoying their light-hearted approach.
	More practical and self-contained than flighty Sagittarius, but also more inclined to worry, you are a naturally attractive individual with a deep sincerity in your relationships.
Sagittarius **Capricorn** Aquarius	Practical Capricorn plus light and airy Sagittarius makes you reliable, although many people find you less accessible, a deep thinker with a light veneer.
	You think deeply about life but are more able to think laterally than other Capricorns, and combine practicality with plenty of charm and more than a little impatience.
Capricorn **Aquarius** Pisces	Add a practical streak of Capricorn to confident Aquarius and you have someone less expressive, perhaps, than a typical Aquarian, but better at getting things done.
	More sincere than you would expect of slightly quirky Aquarius, but flexible and more of a thinker. Also a tendency to be slightly less confident in your ability to charm others.
Aquarius **Pisces** Aries	A good combination. You overlay the sensitive and self-sufficient Pisces with a little more enjoyment of company and confidence to speak your mind, albeit diplomatically.
	Strong and ambitious but sensitive and caring, you have the best of dynamic and forceful Aries combined with unselfish Pisces – as long as they don't pull in opposite directions.

Your very own personal horoscope by **Old Moore**

The timeless wisdom of **Old Moore** *can now be interpreted by computer – to give you an astounding wealth of insights and revelations.*

At last, the huge analytical power of the computer has been harnessed to the legendary forecasting skills of **Old Moore**.

By revealing the mysteries held within your own astrological chart, you will gain a unique insight into yourself and find a new path to your future which you yourself can influence.

It is based on the **Old Moore** prediction system, which has proved to be uniquely successful and accurate for over three hundred years.

Now it focuses entirely on *YOU*. The result is your very own *character profile and forecast horoscope* for the next twelve months.

Send off the coupon below with your remittance of £20.00, and enjoy a unique view of your future.

12-month Horoscope Book
– personal to you – for only £20.00 INCLUDING P&P.

* **Most detailed astral reading of its kind.**

* **CHARACTER PROFILE** explores the depths of your true self.

* **PERSONAL FORECAST** predicts ways to improve your happiness and success.

* *In a tradition of accurate forecasting since 1697.*

YOUR DATE WITH DESTINY...

UNIQUE GIFT IDEA – SEND THIS COUPON NOW!

Your Old Moore Personal Horoscope costs just £20.00 (Please allow 28 days for delivery)

Name ....

Address ....

....

Postcode ....

Telephone ....

Email ....

Date and year of birth ....

Time of birth (if known) ....

Place of birth ....

Use your credit card to order online at www.foulsham.com and enter your date, time and place of birth on the order form.

Or send this completed form to
W. Foulsham & Co. Ltd, Personal Horoscopes, The Old Barrel Store, Drayman's Lane, Marlow, Bucks SL7 2FF.

Please print clearly in BLOCK CAPITALS.

Make cheques payable to W. Foulsham & Co. Ltd.

If you prefer not to receive mailings from companies other than those connected to Old Moore, please tick the box ☐

Gardening by the Moon

In the second century AD, the astronomer Claudius Ptolemy reported of the practical, hard-headed farmers of the Roman Empire that they *'notice the aspects of the Moon, when at full, in order to direct the copulation of their herds and flocks, and the setting of plants or sowing of seeds; and there is not an individual who considers these general precautions as impossible or unprofitable.'*

The idea that the Moon exerts an influence on plant growth is as old as agriculture and embedded in the folklore of many societies. I became intrigued when working on a bio-dynamic farm and decided to investigate the evidence.

The effect of sowing date on crop yield has been thoroughly investigated by the bio-dynamic movement. For some decades, the late Maria Thun reported annual results that show yields varying in accordance with the sidereal zodiac. Recent experiments have shown that the metabolism of plants, indicated by their water absorption or oxygen metabolism, responds considerably to the lunar cycle. University of Paris researchers have demonstrated that plant DNA changes in tune with this cycle. Trees are surrounded by measurable electric fields, monitored for years by Ralph Markson in the US, that demonstrate distinctly lunar rhythms. My own experiments with seeds confirm the results published by Kolisko in the late 1930s and the John Innes Foundation around 1940, that seeds usually germinate better if sown around the Full Moon, and especially on the previous day or two.

Animals coming on heat is also cyclic and traditions link their fertility to the lunar cycle. Data from a thoroughbred stud farm clearly shows both increased fertility and increased coming-on-heat on the days around and just after the Full Moon.

Keys to understanding the relationship of plant response to lunar influence have now emerged and can be incorporated into a gardener's plans as to when best to carry out various tasks. For example, the waning half of the lunar month is best for pruning trees, while the waxing half is better for grafting.

Crops also belong to one of the elements: Earth (Root), Water (Leaf), Air (Flower) or Fire (Fruit-seed). From this it follows that there is a lunar timetable appropriate for each crop. For instance, potatoes, as a Root-crop, grow best when they are sown as the Moon is passing in front of Earth-element constellations.

My book *Gardening and Planting by the Moon* (see page 78) is an invitation to gardeners to investigate the cycles of plant growth, a synthesis of time-honoured traditions and modern research. Totally practical – you need no scientific knowledge – it offers clear explanations followed by a daily calendar outlining the gardening tasks you should focus on to achieve the best results.

I hope that this manual will be used for its practical advantages and as an inspiration to gardeners to become more aware of the life-rhythms in nature which mysteriously connect the growth of plants with cosmic time-cycles.

Nick Kollerstrom

Best Sowing And Planting Times for the Garden in 2019

WHEN TO PLANT OR SOW BY THE MOON TO GET THE BEST RESULTS

Peas, beans, flowering vegetables and plants which produce fruit above the ground should always be sown under a waxing Moon (the period from New Moon to Full). Potatoes and root crops should always be sown when the Moon is low and below the Earth. If you sow, plant or re-pot at the times set out below, it is reasonably certain you will have really fine results. The times are Greenwich Mean Time. Allowances must be made for British Summer Time.

Month	Day	Planting Times		
JANUARY	5, 6, 7 20, 21, 22	8.30 to 11.15 am 8.20 am to 12.05 pm	2.05 to 3.05 pm 1.05 to 2.55 pm	
FEBRUARY	3, 4, 5 18, 19, 20	8.25 to 11.10 am 8.15 am to 10.40 am	12.45 to 3.10 pm 1.10 to 4.00 pm	
		Begin sowing legumes, leaf vegetables and root vegetables. Delay beetroot until the weather is mild. Cut early kidney potatoes for seed and use a heater or heat mats to get them started.		
MARCH	5, 6, 7 20, 21, 22	8.10 am to 12.05 pm 8.05 am to 12.40 pm	1.05 to 2.20 pm 1.40 to 2.55 pm	3.05 to 4.20 pm 3.25 to 4.15 pm
		Planting and sowing into the ground can begin this month. Sow asparagus, celery, brassicas, and continue with root vegetables and legumes. Cabbages, onion sets and sea-kale may be planted out.		
APRIL	4, 5, 6 18, 19, 20	7.20 to 11.45 am 7.45 to 11.20 am	1.05 to 2.45 pm 12.15 to 2.25 pm	4.10 to 5.05 pm 4.05 to 5.45 pm
		Sowing of tomatoes and peppers can begin indoors. Continue sowing legumes, brassicas and leaf vegetables for the main summer crop. Plant out rhubarb, artichokes, asparagus and small salad vegetables. Tie up lettuce and in dry weather water seed in beds.		
MAY	3, 4, 5 17, 18, 19	7.05 to 11.05 am 8.05 am to 12.05 pm	12.30 to 3.10 pm 12.50 to 2.45 pm	4.15 to 6.05 pm 3.50 to 6.00 pm
		Sow cucumber, dwarf bean, runner beans and courgettes and a full crop of kidney beans. Transplant cabbage, winter greens, cauliflower and celery seedlings. Hoe and stake peas, water newly planted crops.		
JUNE	2, 3, 4 17, 18, 19	7.20 to 11.55 am 7.45 to 11.00 am	1.00 to 2.20 pm 12.40 to 3.00 pm	4.15 to 5.35 pm 4.05 to 6.30 pm
		Top beans and peas to assist the filling of the pods. Set kidney beans. Thin out onions, leeks, parsnips and early turnips. Plant tomatoes and peppers outdoors. Water all crops well during dry spells.		
JULY	1, 2, 3 15, 16, 17	6.55 to 11.00 am 7.50 to 11.15 am	1.05 to 3.45 pm 12.40 to 3.15 pm	4.15 to 6.35 pm 4.20 to 7.35 pm
		Plant out the last of the brassicas and cabbages and earth up celery. Lift full-grown winter onions and new potatoes. Pick vine crops as they ripen to encourage new fruit.		
AUGUST	1, 2, 3 14, 15, 16 29, 30, 31	6.30 to 10.00 am 6.55 to 10.55 am 7.15 to 10.35 am	12.30 to 3.00 pm 12.35 to 2.50 pm 12.20 to 2.35 pm	5.55 to 8.00 pm 6.10 to 8.10 pm 6.30 to 8.10 pm
		Sow early cabbages and parsley for the succeeding year, also spinach, broccoli and cauliflower to stand the winter and transplant seedlings. Continue to pick legumes and vine crops as they ripen.		
SEPTEMBER	13, 14, 15 27, 28, 29	7.20 to 11.35 am 7.10 to 11.15 am	1.25 to 4.00 pm 12.55 to 3.20 pm	6.10 to 8.10 pm 5.55 to 7.10 pm
		Plant cabbages, broccoli, cauliflowers, leeks, celery. Pull onions if tips appear to be drying. Sow winter lettuce. Store potatoes and apples properly for winter.		
OCTOBER	12, 13, 14 27, 28, 29	8.45 to 11.00 am 8.15 to 11.35 am	1.00 to 3.25 pm 12.50 to 3.45 pm	4.30 to 6.20 pm 4.40 to 5.40 pm
		Plant some radishes, early cabbages, cauliflower, and some herbs like mint, thyme and tarragon in frames for winter use. Sow the last winter lettuce. Harvest crops before any risk of frost.		
NOVEMBER	12, 13, 14 25, 26, 27	8.10 am to 12.25 pm 8.30 to 11.50 am	1.30 to 4.10 pm 2.15 to 3.20 pm	
		Dig ground once crops are carried off and there is no intention to plant again until spring. Shallots are readily propagated by offcuts. Clear fallen leaves quickly and dispose of diseased plants.		
DECEMBER	11, 12, 13 26, 27, 28	9.10 am to 1.25 pm 8.45 am to 12.20 pm	2.15 to 3.35 pm 2.10 to 2.55 pm	
		Earth up celery. Sow small salad vegetables in warm borders covered with mats.		

Racing with the Jockeys in 2019

ASTROLOGICAL POINTERS TO POSSIBLE WINNING PERIODS

The astrologically compiled dates below are presented to race-goers in the hope that they will point the way to some successful winning periods during the 2019 racing season. Specially recommended = sr.

FAVOURABLE PERIODS FOR FLAT-RACE JOCKEYS

A. KIRBY: Born 22 August 1988. Right-hand courses in the south may bring his best wins this season. His favourable periods are: 8, 10, 24–29 March; 6–11, 13–14, 24–26 April; 2–6, 10, 17–23, 24, 31 May (24 sr); 7–11, 16, 21–24, 30 June; 1, 7, 13–14, 22–23 July (13–14 sr); 3–5, 12–13, 15–20, 26 August (26 sr); 2, 9, 13–17, 24, 30 September (30 sr); 4, 6, 16–17, 20–21, 29 October (20–21 sr); 1, 9–10, 15 November.

L. MORRIS: Born 20 October 1988. Should do especially well on 2- and 3-year-olds at southern meetings. His favourable periods are: 17, 29–30 March; 2–4, 6–9, 14, 26, 29–30 April (29–30 sr); 10–11, 15, 23–27, 31 May (10–11 sr); 6–9, 11–14, 21, 20 June (11–14 sr); 1, 3–4, 11, 17, 22–24 July (14 sr); 1–4, 14, 16–19, 29–31 August (29–31 sr); 2–5, 16, 20–23, 26–28 September (28 sr); 3–6, 12, 18, 20–24, 30 October (30 sr); 2, 4 November.

O. MURPHY: Born 6 September 1995. This rising star ought to be noted this season in the north on longer courses. His favourable periods are: 15, 24, 31 March; 1–2, 5–6, 11–13, 20, 29 April; 4, 7–8, 19–22, 25 May; 10, 13–15, 20, 25–28, 30 June; 4–8, 10–12, 18–20, 25–28 July; 3–8, 10–15, 19–21, 28 August (19–21 sr); 8–9, 15–18, 28–30 September; 9–12, 25–28, 31 October; 1–5, 13–15, 26–28, 30 November (5, 30 sr).

J. FANNING: Born 24 September 1970. This popular Irish jockey should do best on all-weather surfaces this season. His favourable periods are: 23, 26 March; 3–4, 9, 13, 20, 26–28 April (26–28 sr); 2, 6–8, 16, 20–25, 28–30 May (20–25 sr); 13–14, 18, 24–25, 28–30 June; 2–7, 10–11, 18–20, 23, 28–31 July (28–31 sr); 4, 10, 18–19, 27–30 August; 1, 3–4, 7, 13–14, 21, 27, 30 September (21 sr); 1–2, 4–3, 16–18, 22–24 October; 1, 3, 15–16, 26–29 November.

FAVOURABLE PERIODS FOR NATIONAL HUNT JOCKEYS

T. SCUDAMORE: Born 22 May 1982. Should do particularly well in southern steeplechases, rather than hurdles. His favourable periods are: 18, 22–30 January; 1–2, 15–16, 24–27 February; 1–4, 6–7, 27–30 March; 2–3, 7–11, 21–28, 30 April; 7, 13–19, 24, 29 May; 4, 6, 16–20, 29–31 June; 5–7, 16–19, 22–24 July; 2, 6–10, 25–26, 31 August; 2–3, 14–16, 25 September; 1–2, 14–16, 25 October; 2–4, 9–11, 21, 25–29 November (25–29 sr); 12, 16–17, 28 December.

R. JOHNSON: Born 27 July 1977. Ought to succeed best with 3-and 4-year-olds in chases in the Midlands. His favourable periods are: 20–25, 31 January (31 sr); 4–8, 14–17, 21–24 February; 8–10, 11–12, 21–24, 29 March (29 sr); 7–8, 11, 14, 18, 24, 29–30 April (29–30 sr); 1–5, 16, 21, 27 May (21 sr); 3–5, 11, 15–17, 29–30 June; 1–4, 18–19, 29 July; 7–10, 25–25, 31 August; 2–4, 6, 11–12, 27–29 September; 7, 11–13, 27–31 October (31 sr); 1, 5–8, 15–17, 29 November (29 sr); 1, 4–8, 25–27 December.

S. TWISTON DAVIES: Born 15 October 1992. May see his best results in the latter half of the year at southern race tracks. His favourable periods are: 10–13, 16, 12–24 January; 4–5, 9–12, 18–22, 27 February (18–22 sr); 4–9, 19, 20–22, 24–31 March; 2–3, 13, 24–26, 30 April (13 sr); 4, 9, 21–24, 29–31 May; 7, 11–16, 23–24 June; 2–4, 14, 26–31 July (31 sr); 3–5, 14–22, 26–29 August; 2–3, 14–19, 22–27 September; 8–11, 13–18, 22, 26–28 October (26–28 sr); 2–4, 12–15, 23–25 November (23–25 sr); 1–5, 8–10, 12–13, 27 December.

Racing with the Trainers in 2019

ASTROLOGICAL POINTERS TO POSSIBLE WINNING PERIODS

The astrologically compiled dates below are presented to race-goers in the hope that they will point the way to some successful winning periods during the 2019 racing season. Specially recommended = sr.

FAVOURABLE PERIODS FOR FLAT-RACE TRAINERS

J. GOSDEN: Born 30 March 1951. Horses 3 years and over may give the best performances this year. His favourable periods are: 26 March; 10, 12–17, 22–28 April (12 sr); 3–5, 12–16, 22–26 May (16 sr); 2–6, 13, 20, 22–29 June (22–29 sr); 1, 6, 14–16, 22–28 July (22–28 sr); 5, 11–12, 20–26, 28 August (20, 26 sr); 2–7, 12–16, 24, 27–30 September (24 sr); 5, 9–11, 16–17, 24–26 October (24–26 sr); 1–6, 19 November.

M. JOHNSTON: Born 10 October 1959. Should do well with 2-year-olds, particularly at the start of the season. His favourable periods are: 1–3, 8, 11, 19, 30 March; 7–10, 15–16, 17–22, 29 April (15–16 sr); 1–3, 10–11, 16–23, 24 May; 1–3, 6–10, 13–15, 23–27 June (6–10 sr); 4, 7–8, 16–20, 25–26 July; 1, 15–16, 25–29 August; 5–6, 11, 13–16 September (11 sr); 3–6, 9–10, 17–18, 28 October (9–10 sr); 4, 6–10, 13–17, 22–26 November (22–26 sr).

C. APPLEBY: Born 5 July 1975. Could achieve some major victories during the summer, especially in handicaps. His favourable periods are: 14–16, 22, 31 March; 1–4, 11, 18, 28–30 April (28–30 sr); 1–3, 8–10, 14–20, 18–28 May; 2–6, 11–14, 23–30 June; 2–7, 16–18, 28–31 July; 2–3, 11–16, 27–31 August; 4, 13–14, 25, 27–29 September (29 sr); 5–6, 11, 19, 22–24, 31 October (22–24 sr); 1, 8–10 November.

FAVOURABLE PERIODS FOR NATIONAL HUNT TRAINERS

P.F. NICHOLLS: Born 17 April 1962. Courses in the north in the second half of the year may bring best results. His favourable periods are: 14, 19, 22–27 January (22–27 sr); 2, 4–7, 9, 15, 21–22 February; 1, 8–10, 14–16, 28–31 March; 5–7, 16–17, 22–28 April; 1–5, 12, 20–22, 28 May; 4–10, 16, 28–27 June; 2–4, 10–12, 24–26 July; 4–11, 21–22, 27–31 August; 6, 12–18, 28, 30 September; 7–12, 17–20, 25–27, 31 October; 2, 9–15, 28 November (28 sr); 1, 3–8, 10, 17–20 December (17–20 sr).

P. J. HOBBS: Born 26 July 1955. His 3-year-olds early in the year may generate the best results. His favourable periods are: 4, 10, 16–19, 28 January (28 sr); 2–8, 15–16, 25 February (15–16 sr); 4–7, 13–16, 29–31 March; 6, 10–12, 22–25, 30 April (6 sr); 9–13, 16–19, 25–26 May; 12–15, 21, 30 June (30 sr); 4–5, 19–20, 26–31 July; 6–10, 22–25, 31 August (31 sr); 2–4, 15–16, 26 September (2–4 sr); 5, 20–23, 25–26, 31 October (31 sr); 2–6, 23–26 November; 1, 5–6, 14–15, 26–31 December (5–6 sr).

D. McCAIN Jnr: Born 13 June 1970. Ought to excel at races in the Midlands with his 3-year-olds this year. His favourable periods are: 17, 21–25, 31 January; 6, 17–20, 23 February; 1, 6, 17–19, 21–23 March; 7–8, 14, 18–30 April; 1–3, 11, 14–17, 31 May; 1, 13–17, 22–23, 25 June; 5, 15–20, 24–27 July; 2–3, 12–17, 23–27 August (23–27 sr); 2–4, 8, 16–18, 27–28 September (16–18 sr); 1–2, 4–7, 14–18, 17–24, 30 October (14 –18 sr); 7–11, 15–16, 20–21, 25 November (25 sr); 11–13, 22, 28 December (22 sr).

Whatever your star-sign **Old Moore's Horoscope Daily Astral Diary** will guide you through the ups and downs of the coming year.

♈ **ARIES**	21 March	–	20 April
♉ **TAURUS**	21 April	–	21 May
♊ **GEMINI**	22 May	–	21 June
♋ **CANCER**	22 June	–	22 July
♌ **LEO**	23 July	–	23 August
♍ **VIRGO**	24 August	–	23 September
♎ **LIBRA**	24 September	–	22 October
♏ **SCORPIO**	23 October	–	22 November
♐ **SAGITTARIUS**	23 November	–	21 December
♑ **CAPRICORN**	22 December	–	20 January
♒ **AQUARIUS**	21 January	–	19 February
♓ **PISCES**	20 February	–	20 March

These horoscopes are renowned for their accuracy, forward-looking advice and emphasis on planning. With a reading for every day of the year, there is one of these books for each sign of the Zodiac. Let Old Moore help you make the most of 2019.

Available from September (£5.99). For 30% discount, visit www.foulsham.com or call 01256 302699 and quote promotional code 7EP. Also available from good bookshops.

(Please state which sign you require)

Football Pools Forecast for 2019

This forecast, based on a combination of planetary indications and team colours, lists the teams likely to draw on the dates given, or within two days either side. No claims to infallibility are made and readers should use their own judgement, but forecasts may help them in the final selection.

5 January
Brighton, Crystal Palace, Southampton, Charlton Athletic

12 January
Ipswich, Blackpool, Motherwell, Leicester City

19 January
Wigan Portsmouth Middlesbrough Stoke

26 January
West Ham, Watford, Gillingham, Chelsea, Manchester Utd

2 February
Sunderland, Tottenham Hotspur, Fulham, Liverpool

9 February
Huddersfield Town, Celtic, Everton, AFC Bournemouth

16 February
Leicester, Rochdale, Newcastle, Stoke, West Ham

23 February
Chesterfield, Aston Villa, Birmingham, Chelsea

2 March
Reading, Rotherham, QPR, Dundee Utd, Wolverhampton Wanderers

9 March
Swansea, Huddersfield, Hull City, Crystal Palace

16 March
Sheffield Utd, Wimbledon, West Ham, Derby County

23 March
Newcastle, Portsmouth, Gillingham, Dundee, Fulham

30 March
Hull City, Coventry City, Bolton, Sheffield Utd

6 April
Peterborough, Doncaster Rovers, Chelsea, Birmingham, Stoke

13 April
Preston, Ipswich Town, Wolverhampton Wanderers, Charlton Athletic

20 April
Brentford, Charlton Athletic, Hull City, Kilmarnock

27 April
Barnsley, Brighton, AFC Bournemouth, Wigan, Bolton

4 May
Coventry City, Celtic, Blackburn, Sheffield Wednesday

11 May
West Ham, Everton, Hearts, Leeds, West Bromwich Albion, Motherwell

18 May
Sunderland, Colchester Utd, Charlton Athletic, Newcastle

25 May
Bristol City, Sunderland, Rangers, Bradford City, Aston Villa

17 August
St Mirren, Tottenham Hotspur, Ipswich Town, Peterborough

24 August
West Bromwich Albion, Millwall, Fulham, West Ham, Motherwell

31 August
Arsenal, Brentford, Swindon, Cardiff City, Dundee Utd

7 September
Blackpool, Burnley, Manchester Utd, Leicester City, Norwich

14 September
Stoke City, Charlton Athletic, Tottenham Hotspur, Millwall

21 September
Bolton, Manchester Utd, Brighton, West Bromwich Albion, Bury

28 September
Cardiff City, Liverpool, Charlton Athletic, Brighton

5 October
QPR, Blackburn, Burnley, Sheffield Utd, Portsmouth

12 October
Blackpool, Oldham Athletic, Colchester, Tottenham Hotspur

19 October
Manchester City, Newcastle Utd, Oldham Athletic, Barnsley

26 October
Cardiff City, Nottingham Forest, Southampton, Watford

2 November
Brighton, Rangers, Swansea City, AFC Bournemouth, Leicester City

9 November
Norwich, Fulham, Newport, Hull City, Manchester Utd

16 November
Burnley, Shrewsbury Town, Rotherham, Aston Villa

23 November
Bristol City, Chelsea, Norwich, Ipswich, Sunderland

30 November
Newcastle, West Bromwich Albion, Brighton, Sunderland, Manchester City

7 December
Bournemouth, Sunderland, Barnsley, Stoke, Birmingham City

14 December
Doncaster, Chelsea, Southampton, Crystal Palace, Blackpool

21 December
Port Vale, Leeds, Tottenham Hotspur, Preston, Watford, Celtic

28 December
Brighton, Ipswich, Burnley, Crystal Palace, St. Mirren

Who was Old Moore?

Francis Moore, a Shropshire lad, was born in Bridgnorth in 1657, into poverty. Despite his humble beginnings he taught himself to read and write and developed an interest in medicine, which at the time was heavily dependent on astrology.

Realising that Bridgnorth offered insufficient scope for his talent he made his way to London, like Dick Whittington, to make his fortune. Providence gave him the chance of studying with the eminent astrologer John Partridge, who was popular with London's high society. Having added medical astrology to his skills, Dr Francis Moore set up his own business in Southwark. Good at his profession he was privileged to attain the status of Physician to the Court of King Charles II.

Moore launched his first black and white broadsheet in 1697 in support of his Southwark-based apothecary practice – an early advertising campaign! Astrology, combined with his medical advice, was very much in vogue at that time and herbal sales in London shot up. By 1700, with his Court connections, he had compiled the first of his famous *Vox Stellarum* series – *The Voice of the Stars*. The predictions were probably a spin off from his astrological calculations and were included to increase the Almanack sales to a more broadly based public. For those unable to read, special symbols were printed alongside certain days to indicate the importance of the event.

When he died in 1715 Moore's Almanack was taken over by the Worshipful Company of Liveried Stationers who continued to publish it until 1911 when the House of Foulsham bought the copyright. It has been published *every* year since 1697, earning it a place in the *Guinness Book of Records*.

Today a team of astrologers represent Old Moore working 18 months ahead of actual events. They are among the very best and most skilled of UK astrologers. In the Almanack each year Old Moore brings astrological insight into a broad range of editorial features, covering varied subjects from racing to gardening to angling – and not forgetting, of course, the monthly horoscope for each zodiac sign. Why should there be such interest in this simple little book of astrological data and writing? It's down to successful prediction. In the Leader and political editorial which forms the heart of the book, year after year the astrologers describe the direction that the UK and the world will take and generally cover the key players who will take a major role. People keep reading because Old Moore's record is so good they can still use him for their forward planning!

Old Moore predicts modern world affairs with a huge head start. With his historic data records he knows where to look first. There isn't another seer in the world that can claim the duration of accuracy that is published under the by-line Dr Francis Moore.

Angler's Guide for 2019
THE BEST DATES AND TECHNIQUES FOR SUCCESSFUL FISHING

JANUARY: Sport can be hard due to low temperatures, so stick to deeper water on rivers and lakes. Backwaters are a good bet when main rivers are flooded: try float or leger tactics in slack water swims. Shoaling cod may be caught from the beaches, especially in Scotland, on casting gear but they will soon thin out as temperatures rise. **Best days:** 1, 3, 7 (am), 13, 14, 17 (am), 25, 26 (pm), 30 (am).

FEBRUARY: Predator fishing offers the best action with pike, perch and zander all possible on fish baits, but scale down your tackle if the temperature plummets. Big chub can also be had on leger tactics. Spring salmon on the cards for some anglers, but beach rods will have to work harder for their catches. Flatties will still feature, although bigger fish can be had when afloat. **Best days:** 4, 6, 8, 9 (pm), 14, 15 (am), 22, 23, 24, 25 (pm).

MARCH: The freshwater river season closes this month, but almost all commercial still waters will stay open. If mild weather comes early, head for sheltered lakes which can produce superb mixed catches of roach, bream, carp and even tench. Trout anglers head for deep, still waters from the 15th. **Best days:** 1, 2, 3 (pm), 10, 12, 19 (am), 22, 23 (am), 30, 31 (pm).

APRIL: Beach anglers can enjoy the spring run of codling, while those fishing wrecks can expect bumper hauls of pollack, ling and occasional big cod on artificial baits. Ray fishing good, especially in the Solent. Most flies will take trout on still waters but a more careful approach is needed in rivers. **Best days:** 8, 9, 10 (am), 14, 16, 17 (pm), 20, 21, 22 (am), 30 (pm).

MAY: Crab baits worthy for early school bass, flounder and eel, while ragworm and lugworm will take their fair share of plaice in harbours and estuaries. Still-water trout should respond to warmer weather and can be taken on floating lines. Carp will be the bulk of catches for commercial still-water anglers. **Best days:** 5, 6, 7, 9 (am), 13, 15, 16 (pm), 25, 26 (am), 28, 31 (pm).

JUNE: The Glorious 16th will enable specimen tench, carp and bream to be targeted with big baits on both float and leger tackle. Rivers with more pace should provide excellent catches of roach and chub. Beach anglers will find bass more widespread, while their boat counterparts can expect mackerel – the perfect bait for shark and tope – which will start to show off many southern and Welsh ports. **Best days:** 3, 5, 6, 9 (am), 15, 16, 17 (pm), 22, 23 (am), 25, 26, 28 (pm).

JULY: Top sport on rivers and lakes with virtually all species responsive, mostly to particle baits such as corn, hemp and tares. Try swims with plenty of flow as fish, particularly barbel and bream, will be hungry for oxygen-rich water during hot weather. Evening sessions ideal for fly anglers pursuing trout. Shy mullet may be tempted during quiet days around harbours, and bass will be bigger. **Best days:** 11, 12, 13 (pm), 16, 17 (am), 21, 26 (am), 25, 29, 31 (pm).

AUGUST: Low oxygen levels suggest fishing either very early morning or evening periods. Sea anglers afloat can look forward to a multitude of species including bream, bass, pollack, conger and gurnard. Fresh fish baits and crab will outscore all others. **Best days:** 10, 11, 12 (pm), 18, 20 (am), 22, 25 (pm), 27, 28 (am).

SEPTEMBER: Fish will have had time to feed well and big specimens can be expected. Barbel, roach, bream, tench and chub will all be at their optimum weight. Trout anglers may struggle to locate decent fish, although beach and boat rods will be hunting big bass with sand eel baits, crab or lures. **Best days:** 1, 2, 6 (pm), 8, 12, 13 (am), 21, 24 (pm), 26, 29, 30 (pm).

OCTOBER: Cooler temperatures may mean slow sport on lakes, but rivers will be at their peak for roach, chub and dace on caster or maggot. Float tactics are good but don't discount leger or feeder gear. Beach anglers expect the first of the winter codling, where lugworm and squid will be top baits. Extra water may prompt decent catches of salmon for game anglers. **Best days:** 1, 6, 7 (am), 15, 16, 20 (pm), 23, 24 (am), 29, 30, 31 (pm).

NOVEMBER: With shorter days, codling will come closer inshore, especially at deeper venues such as steep beaches, harbour walls and piers. Bad weather may mean slower sport for coarse anglers, who need to scale down hooks and baits. Predator hunters can expect big pike on baits rather than lures. **Best days:** 1, 5, 6, 7 (pm), 15, 17 (am), 21 (pm), 26, 28, 29, 30 (am).

DECEMBER: A roving approach is best during colder weather. Try different swims on backwaters, where roach will take bread flake, and chub can be had on cheese paste, bread, worms and cockles. Pin baits hard to the bottom or let them roll in the flow. After a storm is ideal for targeting codling on beaches, when they attack food stirred up by rough weather. Try night sessions for greater success. **Best days:** 4, 6, 8 (am), 15, 20 (pm), 23 (am), 29, 30, 31 (pm).

Greyhound Racing Numbers for 2019

TRAP-NUMBER FORECASTS FOR POTENTIAL SUCCESS

Each area of the UK has a ruling planetary number and each month of 2019 has a prominent fortunate planetary number. This forecast is based on a combination of those numbers to provide a list of the most propitious dates for betting and the trap numbers most likely to be successful.

The table gives the main areas of the UK and under each monthly heading, the first column shows the best dates for betting, and the second, shaded column gives the trap numbers for the winner and the second dog.

Whilst making no claim to infallibility, this forecast should offer those who enjoy an occasional jaunt to greyhound race meetings a way of aligning their activities with the best planetary influences and potentially increasing their success rate.

MEETING	JAN	FEB	MAR	APRIL	MAY	JUNE	JULY	AUG	SEPT	OCT	NOV	DEC
London	2–8 |45	4–10 |24	2–12 |45	4–10 |24	3–7 |12	4–9 |24	7–12 |23	5–13 |23	2–7 |13	3–12 |14	3–10 |45	2–7 |13
	13–23 |14	13–20 |24	20–23 |12	21–28 |46	18–28 |23	19–27 |15	22–30 |14	17–23 |12	23–28 |13	21–25 |34	18–26 |12	21–26 |24
Birmingham	5–11 |25	1–9 |14	6–11 |13	2–8 |15	5–11 |35	9–13 |25	1–12 |25	3–8 |16	4–9 |13	3–13 |24	10–15 |34	2–7 |36
	13–22 |35	24–28 |23	20–29 |35	12–20 |36	22–28 |25	20–26 |24	23–26 |25	21–28 |23	21–25 |12	20–30 |34	23–31 |15	19–27 |35
Manchester	7–12 |24	3–11 |35	1–6 |17	2–8 |36	4–13 |34	11–14 |25	6–12 |12	7–10 |13	4–8 |23	10–15 |24	1–7 |16	8–12 |34
	16–23 |26	20–27 |34	16–21 |13	17–25 |16	16–21 |45	22–26 |15	16–22 |15	19–27 |34	22–28 |37	26–31 |35	18–24 |46	24–31 |24
Newcastle	8–14 |35	1–5 |15	3–10 |15	10–14 |34	5–13 |15	5–11 |15	5–10 |24	1–9 |12	5–10 |45	8–12 |56	2–10 |13	6–10 |24
	18–21 |1	11–15 |34	15–31 |23	21–26 |14	20–28 |25	21–30 |13	12–27 |24	19–22 |45	24–30 |12	24–28 |35	22–29 |23	22–31 |23
Sheffield	3–8 |25	4–10 |34	1–5 |16	1–6 |24	4–9 |14	3–11 |13	4–11 |26	5–9 |23	1–5 |14	2–9 |23	8–15 |13	7–13 |46
	19–23 |16	14–21 |23	18–31 |3	15–23 |16	18–24 |14	21–24 |45	16–22 |16	18–25 |25	24–30 |13	19–22 |35	21–26 |46	18–21 |24
Wales	2–8 |23	6–13 |15	9–12 |12	6–11 |23	4–10 |14	7–15 |34	8–12 |34	4–8 |15	6–10 |13	2–11 |34	6–12 |23	7–12 |56
	21–26 |12	23–30 |35	21–29 |25	26–30 |14	22–29 |14	16–23 |12	24–31 |25	17–24 |26	23–26 |14	22–30 |36	22–28 |34	20–26 |13
South of England	1–6 |25	9–12 |14	7–13 |23	3–8 |23	4–11 |15	2–7 |56	1–9 |25	9–13 |14	2–12 |25	2–7 |23	8–12 |45	11–15 |14
	23–28 |15	26–30 |25	24–31 |23	21–28 |24	18–26 |16	19–25 |23	19–24 |13	25–31 |23	23–29 |46	23–28 |14	16–23 |35	25–31 |13

Lucky Dates to Play Bingo in 2019

CHECK YOUR ZODIAC SIGN FOR YOUR GOOD-LUCK TIMES

Aries (Birthdays 21 March to 20 April)
13 February to 1 May, 26 June to 2 September, 23 November to 29 December

❖

Taurus (Birthdays 21 April to 21 May)
8 February to 1 April, 27 May to 27 July, 2 October to 30 November

❖

Gemini (Birthdays 22 May to 21 June)
5 February to 27 April, 20 June to 5 August, 3 November to 22 December

❖

Cancer (Birthdays 22 June to 22 July)
19 January to 13 March, 28 July to 18 September, 15 November to 16 December

❖

Leo (Birthdays 23 July to 23 August)
13 January to 24 March, 29 May to 1 August, 9 October to 28 November

❖

Virgo (Birthdays 24 August to 23 September)
5 February to 24 May, 2 July to 15 August, 29 October to 10 December

❖

Libra (Birthdays 24 September to 23 October)
18 January to 12 March, 7 May to 4 July, 8 November to 31 December

❖

Scorpio (Birthdays 24 October to 22 November)
2 March to 29 May, 25 June to 18 August, 2 October to 26 November

❖

Sagittarius (Birthdays 23 November to 21 December)
19 January to 11 March, 20 July to 20 September, 2 November to 28 December

❖

Capricorn (Birthdays 22 December to 20 January)
5 March to 19 April, 7 June to 16 August, 24 September to 25 November

❖

Aquarius (Birthdays 21 January to 19 February)
4 February to 22 March, 14 May to 25 July, 22 October to 8 December

❖

Pisces (Birthdays 20 February to 20 March)
9 February to 20 April, 7 July to 29 August, 29 October to 15 December

Thunderball Astro-Guide for 2019

Thunderball forecasts are based on the power of the Sun and Jupiter in each zodiacal period. In a random draw there can be no guarantee, but these numbers may help to improve your chances. First, find your sun sign in the left-hand column. Then read across the first panel to select five numbers 1–39 for the main part of your entry. Then select one number from the second panel for the Thunderball.

Sign		Main numbers						Thunderball			
ARIES 21 MARCH TO 20 APRIL	5	6	8	12	29	39	1	7	10	13
TAURUS 21 APRIL TO 21 MAY	1	3	15	19	27	34	2	4	5	12
GEMINI 22 MAY TO 21 JUNE	10	14	22	27	29	35	2	3	8	9
CANCER 22 JUNE TO 22 JULY	7	12	19	24	33	38	9	10	11	12
LEO 23 JULY TO 23 AUGUST	5	6	18	19	31	37	2	3	6	13
VIRGO 24 AUGUST TO 23 SEPTEMBER	10	19	23	24	26	35	1	5	10	11
LIBRA 24 SEPTEMBER TO 23 OCTOBER	8	11	25	26	34	37	4	5	7	13
SCORPIO 24 OCTOBER TO 22 NOVEMBER	7	17	27	28	34	35	2	6	8	10
SAGITTARIUS 23 NOVEMBER TO 21 DECEMBER	10	16	20	30	33	39	1	5	7	11
CAPRICORN 22 DECEMBER TO 20 JANUARY	9	11	22	28	30	34	3	4	9	12
AQUARIUS 21 JANUARY TO 19 FEBRUARY	7	14	22	23	25	35	2	8	12	13
PISCES 20 FEBRUARY TO 20 MARCH	5	10	12	21	27	32	7	9	10	13

Your Lucky Lotto

The prevailing planetary influences are the basis for this astro-guide to lucky Lotto numbers in 2019. Any Lotto forecast must be fallible, but to give yourself the best chance of winning, refer to the section on your birth sign.

 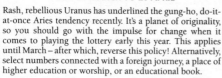

ARIES

BORN 21 MARCH TO 20 APRIL

Rash, rebellious Uranus has underlined the gung-ho, do-it-at-once Aries tendency recently. It's a planet of originality, so you should go with the impulse for change when it comes to playing the lottery early this year. This applies until March – after which, reverse this policy! Alternatively, select numbers connected with a foreign journey, a place of higher education or worship, or an educational book.

3	4	10	18	27	31	43	45	51	54
7	9	22	23	36	38	48	49	55	58

 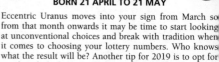

TAURUS

BORN 21 APRIL TO 21 MAY

Eccentric Uranus moves into your sign from March so from that month onwards it may be time to start looking at unconventional choices and break with tradition when it comes to choosing your lottery numbers. Who knows what the result will be? Another tip for 2019 is to opt for numbers linked to your bank account (whether single or joint), your tax or NI details.

2	8	17	18	27	30	40	42	47	50
9	10	20	26	35	38	45	45	53	56

LEO

BORN 23 JULY TO 23 AUGUST

Leos often live to impress others, and thus it is with your spending habits too. Perhaps experiment with a new strategy this year: select a set of numbers for one month, change them the next month, change them again the following month and so on. You may find your luck changes with you! Alternatively, if this doesn't suit you, choose numbers that are linked to your partner or spouse, a creative project or your children.

1	5	10	15	23	24	32	33	42	50
6	7	16	19	25	26	34	41	52	59

VIRGO

BORN 24 AUGUST TO 23 SEPTEMBER

Fantasy-prone Neptune is still in your opposite sign (Pisces) suggesting you should heed your *own* advice when making important decisions. This applies to the lottery, too. Stick to whatever method has worked in the past, but try to avoid being purely random when choosing numbers. In other words, have a system. For example, this year you should select numbers linked to your present home, your childhood, or your parents.

3	4	12	13	21	22	30	31	49	51
6	9	15	18	24	27	42	45	57	58

SAGITTARIUS

BORN 23 NOVEMBER TO 21 DECEMBER

Your ruling planet Jupiter, associated with good fortune, comes home to roost this year – and this won't just apply to the lottery. Up the stakes if you can to give yourself a better chance of winning. If you are choosing new numbers for the next twelve months, try those that are linked to a personal detail about yourself, for example your age this year, your height, weight, or shoe size perhaps.

1	3	12	15	21	23	33	36	50	51
6	9	18	19	27	28	45	46	54	55

CAPRICORN

BORN 22 DECEMBER to 20 JANUARY

With hard-nosed Saturn returning to its native sign of Capricorn this year, it's time to embrace all things traditional. This could be the year to stick with the same number choices – don't deviate, keep things the same and who knows? When you are making your initial choice, try numbers that are linked to your recent past, a medical issue (such as hospital reference number, doctor's phone number) or even a sea voyage you've taken.

2	3	12	17	30	35	39	41	48	49
5	8	21	26	36	37	44	47	52	53

Astro-guide for 2019

Choose two numbers from the first square, then one number from each of the following squares. Either keep to the same numbers each week or vary the astrological indicators according to your personal vibrations.

USING THIS SYSTEM READER WINS **£40,000** MRS THERESE SINGER OF GLASGOW

GEMINI
BORN 22 MAY TO 21 JUNE

Satisfy your love of change over the coming twelve months by keeping your lottery numbers different each week and his could be the year when your money pot expands! Playing with others in a duo (especially close partners) may also enhance your chances. Your luck may also be boosted this year if you choose digits that represent your spouse, partner, best friend or even a business associate such as birthdays, anniversaries or house numbers.

3	5	14	16	25	27	32	34	43	48
7	12	21	23	28	30	39	41	50	52

CANCER
BORN 22 JUNE TO 22 JULY

Attached to the past as you are, you may prefer to keep to a certain set of regular numbers when you play the lottery. This would certainly be playing to your strengths this year, when repetition and consistency work for you. If however you need to change your regular numbers, choose figures associated with your place of work (or a colleague), your doctor or even a pet.

2	4	9	13	20	22	31	33	42	44
6	8	15	17	24	26	35	40	56	58

LIBRA
BORN 24 SEPTEMBER TO 23 OCTOBER

Originality may be the key to Libra's winning strategy this year; if you usually keep to a set of numbers, change them at random and listen to your intuition instead. It's said that luck is often self-created, and this may be the way ahead for Libra in the coming twelve months. You may also consider selecting numbers related to your primary/secondary school or a means of transport – your car, train or bus journey for instance.

1	3	10	12	21	25	34	39	52	53
7	8	16	17	28	30	43	48	57	59

SCORPIO
24 OCTOBER TO 22 NOVEMBER

Wild Uranus enters your house of relationships this year, which is an indicator that you should consider avoiding syndicates or sharing tickets with your partner, and instead heed your own intuition. The reason? The planet of Luck, Jupiter, is passing through your solar money house and this may lead to a desire to throw caution to the wind in many types of financial speculation. Choose numbers connected to personal finance, your bank or building society.

1	2	17	20	29	35	38	44	53	55
8	10	25	27	36	37	46	47	56	57

AQUARIUS
BORN 21 JANUARY TO 19 FEBRUARY

The key to understanding Aquarians is to recognise their love of teamwork – and this is exactly how you should play the lottery this year as syndicates are favourably highlighted. It may also be a good idea to find new ways of choosing your numbers. Consider figures associated with a particular social group, club, or meeting place if you have one; if not numbers connected in some way with an old friend.

2	4	11	13	20	22	32	38	47	55
5	6	14	15	23	24	40	41	56	57

PISCES
BORN 20 FEBRUARY TO 20 MARCH

Your ruler Neptune – also the planet of big dreams – is moving through your sign for the next twelve months. Your best bet is to take a flexible approach to your lottery numbers – take a new approach or even consider numbers connected with your actual night-time dreams! Alternatively, choose numbers related to your professional situation or career in any way you can think of, from your office phone number to your boss's birthday.

1	3	10	12	19	22	31	40	55	56
4	9	13	18	29	30	49	54	58	59

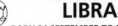

Euro Millions Astro-indicator for 2019

Twelve has always been the perfect 'cyclical' number and is the 'pool' from which you can select from numbers below – they may help to improve your chances. Find your sun sign in the left-hand column, then read across the first panel and choose five numbers (1–50) for the main board. Then two for the Lucky Star section on the right. Some will overlap.

Sign			Main board (1–50)						Lucky Star			
ARIES 21 March to 20 April	7	15	18	21	29	33	46	48	1	2	3	12
TAURUS 21 April to 21 May	2	9	17	18	22	24	30	40	1	5	6	11
GEMINI 22 May to 21 June	4	7	18	34	35	38	41	49	2	4	8	10
CANCER 22 June to 22 July	12	22	24	29	33	41	44	48	3	6	9	10
LEO 23 July to 23 August	9	13	19	32	35	40	42	44	4	8	11	12
VIRGO 24 August to 23 September	2	11	23	27	31	44	46	50	3	5	8	12
LIBRA 24 September to 23 October	2	10	18	34	37	40	45	46	5	6	7	11
SCORPIO 24 October to 22 November	6	11	17	18	25	39	47	50	4	8	9	11
SAGITTARIUS 23 November to 21 December	3	9	11	26	30	45	47	48	1	3	9	10
CAPRICORN 22 December to 20 January	13	21	22	27	30	33	41	44	2	4	5	6
AQUARIUS 21 January to 19 February	1	2	5	21	23	25	48	49	2	7	8	9
PISCES 20 February to 20 March	1	3	16	19	30	38	42	47	1	3	4	5

gardening & planting by the **moon** 2019

BBC lunar gardening correspondent and high-profile author Nick Kollerstrom presents this complete guide to gardening in harmony with the rhythm of the moon. Gardeners at RHS Wisley have proved the benefits of the lunar effect, which produces higher yields and better flavour in vegetables, and stronger, more colourful flower beds. Everything you need to know about the position of the moon and the planets through the year is here, plus a 15-month calendar and timetable.

£8.99

Published: August 2018

978-0-572-04747-4   30% discount on-line at www.foulsham.com or by calling 01256 302699 with code OM9.

Health Lottery Astro-Guide for 2019

Health Lottery forecasts are based on the strength of Jupiter and planetary associations with the solar sixth house. These aspects are traditionally connected to health matters, whilst Jupiter signifies good luck generally. The numbers below may help to improve your chances at winning: just find your sun sign, then select three numbers 1–50 from the first panel. Then choose two from the second 1–30.

Sign	Dates	First panel (1–50)	Second panel (1–30)
ARIES	21 March to 20 April	8 11 35 38 42 43	4 12 21 29
TAURUS	21 April to 21 May	4 15 16 29 38 46	11 12 20 30
GEMINI	22 May to 21 June	10 26 27 36 39 50	12 22 27 28
CANCER	22 June to 22 July	1 16 23 30 44 45	2 17 20 25
LEO	23 July to 23 August	13 15 24 25 42 44	8 10 24 30
VIRGO	24 August to 23 September	8 17 23 28 38 42	3 13 19 26
LIBRA	24 September to 23 October	7 10 24 34 40 43	2 6 18 27
SCORPIO	24 October to 22 November	9 10 21 33 34 46	3 7 9 29
SAGITTARIUS	23 November to 21 December	14 17 22 25 37 43	1 6 18 25
CAPRICORN	22 December to 20 January	13 15 20 31 40 43	8 11 19 23
AQUARIUS	21 January to 19 February	8 16 32 37 44 50	4 6 16 30
PISCES	20 February to 20 March	2 13 22 33 42 47	14 17 25 26

UK Fairs and Events 2019

*Dates may be based on traditional fixtures and both dates and venues are subject to change.
Always check local press or with organisers well in advance.*

AGRICULTURAL AND COUNTRYSIDE

Anglesey County Show: Gwalchmai 13–14 August

Appleby Horse Fair: Appleby-in-Westmorland, Cumbria 6–12 June

Bakewell Show: 7–8 August

Bingley Show: Myrtle Park, Bingley 20 July

Black Isle Show: Mansfield Showground, Muir of Ord 1 August

Border Union Show: Springwood Park, Kelso 26–27 July

Cheshire County Show: Tabley, Nr Knutsford 18–19 June

Country Fest: Westmorland County Showground, Lane Farm, Crooklands, Milnthorpe 1–2 June

Countryside Live: Great Yorkshire Showground, Harrogate 19–20 October

Cumberland County Show: Rickerby Park, Carlisle 8 June

Denbigh and Flint Show: The Green, Denbigh 15 August

Derbyshire County Show: Elvaston, Nr Derby 23 June

Devon County Show: Westpoint, Clyst St Mary, Exeter 16–18 May

Dorset County Show: Dorchester Showground 7–8 September

Dumfries and Lockerbie Agricultural Show: Park Farm, Dumfries 3 August

East of England Autumn Show: Showground, Peterborough 13 October

East of England Show and Just Dogs Live: Showground, Peterborough 5–7 July

Edenbridge and Oxted Agricultural Show: Ardenrun Showground, Lingfield 26 August

Eye Show: Goodrich Park, Palgrave 25–26 August

Great Yorkshire Show: Great Yorkshire Showground, Harrogate 9–11 July

Hertfordshire County Show: The Showground, Redbourn 25–26 May

Kelso Ram Sales: Springwood Park 13 September

Kent County Show: Detling, Maidstone 5–7 July

Lincolnshire Show: Grange-de-Lings, Lincoln 19–20 June

Monmouthshire Show: Vauxhall Fields, Monmouth 29 August

Nantwich Show and International Cheese Awards: Dorfold Hall Park, Nantwich 31 July

New Forest and Hampshire County Show: New Park, Brockenhurst 23–25 July

Newark and Nottinghamshire County Show: Newark Showground, Newark-on-Trent 11–12 May

Newark Vintage Tractor and Heritage Show: Showground, Newark-on-Trent 9–10 November

North Somerset Show: Bathing Pond Fields, Wraxall, Nr Bristol 6 May

Northumberland County Show: Bywell, Nr Stocksfield 27 May

Oxfordshire County and Thame Show: Thame Showground 27 July

Pembrokeshire County Show: Withybush, Haverfordwest 20–22 August

Romsey Show: Broadlands, Romsey 14 September

Royal Bath & West AMES: Showground, Shepton Mallet 6 February

Royal Bath & West Dairy Show: Showground, Shepton Mallet 2 October

Royal Bath & West Show: Showground, Shepton Mallet 29 May–1 June

Royal Cornwall Show: Wadebridge 6–8 June

Royal County of Berkshire Show: Newbury Showground 21–22 September

Royal Highland Show: Ingliston, Edinburgh 20–23 June (provisional)

Royal Norfolk Show: Norfolk Showground, Norwich 26–27 June

Royal Welsh Show: Llanelwedd, Builth Wells 22–25 July

Royal Welsh Winter Fair: Llanelwedd, Builth Wells 25–26 November

Shire Horse Society Spring Show: Arena UK Showground, Allington 15–17 March

Shropshire County Show: West Midlands Agricultural Showground, Shrewsbury 18 May

South of England Autumn Show and Game Fair: SoE Centre, Haywards Heath 5–6 October

South of England Show: South of England Centre, Ardingly, Haywards Heath 6–8 June

Staffordshire County Show: Stafford Showground 29–30 May

Suffolk Show: Trinity Park, Ipswich 29–30 May

Surrey County Show: Stoke Park, Guildford 27 May

Tendring Hundred Show: Lawford House Park, Nr Manningtree 13 July

Three Counties Show: Three Counties Showground, Malvern 14–16 June
Turriff Show: The Showground, Turriff, Aberdeenshire 3–4 Aug
Westmorland County Show: Lane Farm, Crooklands 12 September

OTHER EVENTS

Badminton Horse Trials: 1–5 May
BBC Gardeners' World Live: NEC Birmingham 13–16 June (provisional)
Blackpool Illuminations: 30 August–3 November
Border Union Championship Dog Show: Springwood Park, Kelso 15–16 June
Braemar Gathering: 7 September
Burghley Horse Trials: Burghley Park, Stamford 5–8 September
Chester Folk Festival: Kelsall 27 May
Cowes Week: 10–17 August
Crufts Dog Show: NEC Birmingham 7–10 March
Edinburgh International Festival: 2–26 August
Edinburgh Military Tattoo: Edinburgh Castle Esplanade 2–24 August
Glastonbury Festival: 26–30 June
Golf. British Open Championship: Royal Portrush 18–21 July. **Women's British Open**: Lytham St Annes 2–5 August. **Amateur**: Portmarnock & The Island 17–22 June. **Boys Amateur**: Saunton East and West 13–18 August. **Seniors Amateur**: North Berwick 31 July–2 August. **Seniors Open**: Lytham St Annes 25–28 July. **Boys Home Internationals**: Ashburnham 6–8 August.
Hay Festival: Hay-on-Wye 23 May–2 June
Helston Furry Dance: 8 May
Henley Regatta: 3–7 July
The Hoppings (funfair): Town Moor, Newcastle 21–29 June
Horse Racing. Cheltenham Gold Cup: 15 March. **Grand National**: Aintree 6 April. **Scottish Grand National**: Ayr 13 April. **2000 Guineas**: Newmarket 4 May (prov.). **Epsom Derby**: 1 June. **Royal Ascot**: 20–24 June. **Glorious Goodwood**: 30 July–3 August (prov.). **St Leger**: Doncaster 14 September (prov). **King George VI Chase**: Kempton 26 December.
Hull Fair: 4–12 October
Isle of Man TT Races: Douglas, IoM 25 May–7 June
Isle of Wight Festival: Seaclose Park, Newport, Isle of Wight 20–23 June
Jersey Battle of Flowers: 8–9 August
Leeds Festival: Bramham Park 23–25 August
Llangollen International Musical Eisteddfod: 9–14 July

London to Brighton Veteran Car Run: Hyde Park, London–Madeira Drive, Brighton 3 November (provisional)
London Harness Horse Parade: South of England Showground, Ardingly, Haywards Heath 22 April
London Marathon: Greenwich Park–The Mall, London 28 April
London Motor Show: Battersea Park 16–19 May
Lord Mayor's Show: City of London 9 November
Military Odyssey: Kent County Showground, Detling, Maidstone 24–26 August
Nottingham Goose Fair: 2–6 October (traditional fixture; check local press)
Notting Hill Carnival: 25–26 August
'Obby 'Oss Day (May Day): Padstow, 1 May
Oxford vs Cambridge Boat Race: River Thames, Putney–Mortlake 7 April
Ould Lammas Fair: Ballycastle 26–27 August
Palace to Place Cycle Ride: Buckingham Palace–Windsor Castle 6 October (provisional)
Reading Festival: Richfield Avenue 23–25 August
RHS Chelsea Flower Show: 21–25 May (RHS members only first two days. Advance booking required.)
RHS Flower Show: Bute Park, Cardiff 12–14 April
RHS Flower Show: Chatsworth Estate, Derbyshire 5–9 June
RHS Flower Show: Tatton Park, Nr Knutsford, Cheshire 17–21 July
RHS Hampton Court Palace Flower Show: 2–7 July (RHS members only first two days. Advance booking required.)
RHS Malvern Autumn Show: Three Counties Showground 28–29 September
RHS Malvern Spring Show: Three Counties Showground 9–12 May
RideLondon: London–Surrey 27–28 July (provisional)
Royal International Air Tattoo: RAF Fairford, Gloucestershire 19–21 July
Royal Windsor Horse Show: Home Park, Windsor 8–12 May
Shrewsbury Folk Festival: 23–26 August
Shropshire County Horse Show: West Midlands Agricultural Showground, Shrewsbury 18 May
Sidmouth Folk Week: 2–9 August
Trooping the Colour: Horse Guards Parade, London 8 June
Three Choirs Festival: Gloucester 27 July–3 August
Three Counties Championship Dog Show: Malvern Showground, Malvern 6–9 June
Up Helly Aa (fire festival and torchlight parade): Lerwick, Shetland Isles 31 January
Whitby Folk Festival: 24–30 August
Wimbledon Lawn Tennis Championships: 1–14 July

Lighting-up Times for 2018

Vehicle lamps must be used between sunset and sunrise. Times are in GMT, except 01.00 on 25 March to 01.00 on 28 October when they are BST (1 hour in advance). They are calculated for London (longitude 0º, latitude N.51º5).

Day	January h m	February h m	March h m	April h m	May h m	June h m	July h m	August h m	September h m	October h m	November h m	December h m
1	16 31	17 19	18 10	20 03	20 53	21 37	21 50	21 19	20 17	19 09	17 04	16 25
2	16 32	17 21	18 11	20 04	20 54	21 38	21 50	21 17	20 15	19 06	17 02	16 24
3	16 34	17 23	18 13	20 06	20 56	21 40	21 50	21 15	20 13	19 04	17 00	16 24
4	16 35	17 24	18 15	20 08	20 58	21 41	21 49	21 14	20 10	19 02	16 58	16 23
5	16 36	17 26	18 17	20 39	20 59	21 41	21 49	21 12	20 08	18 59	16 57	16 23
6	16 37	17 28	18 18	20 11	21 01	21 42	21 48	21 10	20 06	18 57	16 55	16 22
7	16 38	17 30	18 20	20 13	21 02	21 43	21 48	21 08	20 04	18 55	16 53	16 22
8	16 40	17 32	18 22	20 14	21 04	21 44	21 47	21 06	20 01	18 53	16 52	16 22
9	16 41	17 34	18 24	20 16	21 06	21 45	21 46	21 05	19 59	18 51	16 50	16 21
10	16 43	17 35	18 25	20 18	21 07	21 46	21 46	21 03	19 57	18 48	16 48	16 21
11	16 44	17 37	18 27	20 19	21 09	21 46	21 45	21 01	19 55	18 46	16 47	16 21
12	16 45	17 39	18 29	20 21	21 10	21 47	21 44	20 59	19 52	18 44	16 45	16 21
13	16 47	17 41	18 31	20 23	21 12	21 48	21 43	20 57	19 50	18 42	16 44	16 21
14	16 48	17 43	18 32	20 24	21 13	21 48	21 42	20 55	19 48	18 40	16 43	16 21
15	16 50	17 45	18 34	20 26	21 15	21 49	21 41	20 53	19 45	18 37	16 41	16 21
16	16 51	17 46	18 36	20 28	21 16	21 49	21 40	20 51	19 43	18 35	16 40	16 21
17	16 53	17 48	18 37	20 30	21 18	21 50	21 39	20 49	19 41	18 33	16 38	16 21
18	16 55	17 50	18 39	20 31	21 19	21 50	21 38	20 47	19 38	18 31	16 37	16 22
19	16 56	17 52	18 41	20 33	21 21	21 50	21 37	20 45	19 36	18 29	16 36	16 22
20	16 58	17 54	18 43	20 35	21 22	21 51	21 36	20 43	19 34	18 27	16 35	16 22
21	17 00	17 55	18 44	20 36	21 24	21 51	21 34	20 41	19 31	18 25	16 34	16 23
22	17 01	17 57	18 46	20 38	21 25	21 51	21 33	20 39	19 29	18 23	16 33	16 23
23	17 03	17 59	18 48	20 40	21 26	21 51	21 32	20 37	19 27	18 21	16 31	16 24
24	17 05	18 01	18 49	20 41	21 28	21 51	21 31	20 35	19 25	18 19	16 30	16 24
25	17 06	18 03	19 51	20 43	21 29	21 51	21 29	20 32	19 22	18 17	16 29	16 25
26	17 08	18 04	19 53	20 44	21 30	21 51	21 28	20 30	19 20	18 15	16 29	16 26
27	17 10	18 06	19 54	20 41	21 32	21 51	21 26	20 28	19 18	18 13	16 28	16 27
28	17 12	18 08	19 56	20 48	21 33	21 51	21 25	20 26	19 15	18 11	16 27	16 27
29	17 14		19 58	20 49	21 34	21 51	21 23	20 24	19 13	17 09	16 26	16 28
30	17 15		19 59	20 51	21 35	21 51	21 22	20 22	19 11	17 07	16 25	16 29
31	17 17		20 01		21 36		21 20	20 19		17 05		16 30